POOL

Private Pilots Guide

CW00585386

Understanding Weather
for Sport Pilots

David Cockburn

Nothing in this book supersedes any legislation, rules, regulations or procedures contained in any operational document issued by Her Majesty's Stationery Office, the Civil Aviation Authority, the European Aviation Safety Agency, ICAO, the manufacturers of aircraft, engines and systems, or by the operators of aircraft throughout the world.

Understanding Weather for Sport Pilots - David Cockburn

© David Cockburn 2008

ISBN 978-1-84336-154-1

Pooleys Flight Equipment Ltd
Elstree Aerodrome
Hertfordshire
WD6 3AW
England

Tel: 0208 953 4870
Fax: 0208 953 2512
www.pooleys.com
sales@pooleys.com

Preface

This book has been produced primarily to assist microlight pilots by giving them a document to which they can refer in order to achieve safe and practical flights. It is as relevant to those flying modern, fast, light aeroplanes as to those with weight-shift machines, and should be useful for any sport aviator, whatever he or she may fly.

Aircraft handling skills can be learned, and pilots are (or ought to be) in control over how they use these skills. However, no-one has control at all over what Nature may produce, and as many have found, it is easy for the weather to gain the better of a pilot. For that reason, the book contains a certain amount of basic theory as a background to its important guidance on obtaining and using the available meteorological information. It also contains much practical advice on how to recognise and avoid potential weather hazards.

It is sometimes said that a butterfly flapping its wings in the Amazon rainforest will eventually affect the weather in the British Isles. The atmosphere will very seldom act exactly as this or any book suggests, and pilots are unlikely to see any weather feature exactly as the descriptions, but the general trends and principles will nearly always apply. Modern meteorological forecasts are produced by computer with guidance from highly trained and qualified scientists, but these forecasts can never be completely accurate, and are certainly not tailored to the requirements of an individual pilot. To enjoy our flying to the maximum while retaining a reasonable level of safety, we need to learn as much about the weather as possible. We should make an effort to interpret published forecasts, and then compare these forecasts and our interpretations with what actually happens later.

This book of course can only act as an introduction to the subject of meteorology. Hopefully, it will encourage readers to consult more detailed books on the subject to improve their knowledge

The author is grateful for the assistance of the UK Met Office, with whose permission many of the charts have been reproduced.

In this document, the male pronoun 'he' is often used to refer to both genders. This is no slight on the ladies who fly, merely a space saving and readability measure.

Editorial Team

AUTHOR David Cockburn

David Cockburn has been flying light aircraft since 1965. While serving in the Royal Air Force as a pilot and flying instructor, much of his spare time was taken up with the sport of gliding. He became a gliding instructor in 1967, and served several times as club Chief Instructor. He has competed in gliding competitions in the UK and Europe and obtained the FAI Diamond gliding badge in 1976. Towards the end of his RAF career, he amassed over 1000 hours flying and instructing on Chipmunk aircraft and currently instructs at flying clubs on a variety of light aircraft, as well a writing books on aviation subjects, including all the PPL ground subjects.

While talking to pilots of microlight and other light sport aircraft, it seemed that many had a limited knowledge of weather, despite its considerable effect on them. This may have been because the available books on the subject were either too sketchy or too oriented towards examinations. He therefore decided to make use of his gliding and instructional experience to write this book, which leads the reader in a logical fashion through the aspects of the subject most relevant to them.

Daljeet Gill

Daljeet is Head of Design & Development for Pooleys Flight Equipment and editor of the Pooleys Private Pilots Guides, Pre-flight Briefing, R/T Communications, Pooleys ATPL Manuals and Air Presentation, Ground School Training Transparencies plus many others. Daljeet has been involved with editing, typesetting and design for all these publications. Graduated in 1999 with a BA (hons) in Graphic Design, she deals with marketing, advertising & design of our new products. She maintains our website and produces our Pooleys Catalogue annually.

Contents

Intentionally Left Blank

Chapter 1

Heat in the Atmosphere

1.1 Introduction

Our earth is surrounded by air, its 'atmosphere'. The movement of that atmosphere, and the changes to the substances composing it, produce our weather. These movements and changes are caused by variations in the amount of heat, normally measured as temperature, in that atmosphere. "Meteorology" is learning how temperature changes happen, and their consequences.

1.2 The Atmosphere

Nearly all the atmosphere is in gas form, clear and transparent. Any lack of that clarity is caused by some liquid, or solid particles, being suspended in that gas. Although many different gases are found in the atmosphere, only a few occur in significant quantities at the levels light aircraft fly.

Most (78%) of the atmosphere is Nitrogen (N_2), and about 20% is Oxygen (O_2). The remainder is mainly made up of Carbon Dioxide (CO_2) and water vapour (H_2O) in varying amounts. Water vapour is indeed a gas; it is when that gas changes to liquid that most of our "weather" is produced.

The gas atoms of the atmosphere have mass. The earth's gravity affects all of them, and the atoms of the air at the 'top' of the atmosphere push down on the atoms below them, which push down on those below them in turn, progressively compressing the air as it becomes closer to the earth's surface. The higher atoms are far apart, with little 'pressure', but the compressed atoms close to the earth are closer together, or 'denser', with a much greater pressure.

1.3   Heating from the Sun

Although a small amount of heat energy reaches the earth's surface from inside, by volcanic action, virtually all the atmospheric heating originates from the sun. The sun produces (radiates) a vast amount of energy, which can be felt as heat when it strikes objects. Solid objects are easily heated by direct sunlight, but gases are affected by only some parts of the direct radiation.

The very low density of atoms at the top of the atmosphere, virtually in space, absorb some of the energy (also sometimes called 'cosmic rays') as heat. However, the rays which pass through to the lower layer of the atmosphere are of a form which has little direct effect on gases, so we must consider the earth's surface.

The earth is a spheroid (a slightly squashed sphere). The sun's rays strike the middle of it directly, but only strike the areas closer to the poles at shallow angles. These polar areas receive much less energy, so less heat, than those near the equator. The earth spins, so whichever point the rays strike the earth normally receives more energy at midday than in the morning or the evening, and none at night. This is called a 'diurnal' variation, meaning 'over the course of 24 hours'.

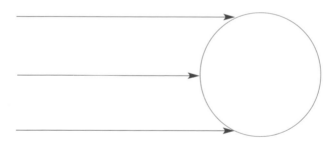

FIGURE 1.1 SOLAR RADIATION ON THE EARTH

However, the earth does not spin in an upright position relative to the sun. The axis around which it spins is offset, as shown in figure 1.2. As the earth travels round the sun every year, the sun appears to move north and south, reaching its maximum northerly point in June, its maximum southerly point in December, and crossing the equator every March and September. Areas around the poles have periods when no heat reaches them (Arctic winter). This is a 'seasonal' variation.

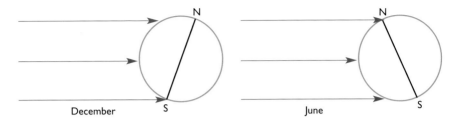

FIGURE 1.2 SEASONAL VARIATION

1.4   The Effect of Clouds

Clouds consist of drops of water, through which the sun's rays do not pass directly. A very small amount of energy is absorbed by the liquid water, but the main effect is to "diffract" or 'spread out' the energy, some being reflected away from the earth entirely. The light from the sun illustrates this diffraction to some extent; the thicker the cloud, the less energy reaches the earth's surface.

1.5   Surface Warming

The energy that does reach the surface of the earth heats different parts to a different extent, depending on various factors. The angle at which it meets the surface is important, as seen already. Sloping ground absorbs more heat when the sun's rays strike against the slope than along it.

The amount of heat absorbed also depends on what is absorbing it. An area of water reflects some of the energy, but whatever is left is usually absorbed within a layer a few feet below the water surface; shallow water allows some heat to pass through to the beach beneath. The energy absorbed by solid ground is normally absorbed in a much thinner layer, a matter of inches thick.

The colour and shade of an object affects the amount of heat it absorbs, and the rate of absorption. A white object tends to reflect much of the heat energy, while a dark object tends to absorb more. The composition of the surface also affects the heating. Sand or soil allows much of the energy to pass between the grains, and the layer heated is thicker than that of a solid surface, a concrete road for example. The thickness of the heated layer does not actually affect the amount of heat absorbed, but it does affect the temperature which we would measure on the surface.

1.6   Re-radiation

Having been heated by the sun, the earth continually radiates some of that heat energy back out into space. Again, a little is absorbed by the gases in the atmosphere, and much is reflected back again by cloud, but both effects are now more pronounced than when the shorter wavelength rays from the sun pass through it. The combination of daytime heating and continuous re-radiation means that points on the earth are normally coldest shortly after dawn and warmest about two hours after local noon. This diurnal variation in temperature is the trigger for other changes, seen later.

However, we can consider that the air in the lower part of the atmosphere, the 'troposphere', gains virtually all its heat energy in a different fashion.

1.7   Convection

The air in contact with a warm surface itself becomes warmer, by 'conduction'. Because the surface is warmed unequally, pockets of warmer air form, being surrounded by slightly cooler air. The warmer air expands compared to its environment, and becomes lighter. The lighter air rises, and so spreads warmth upwards by 'convection'.

The rising air moves upwards into an environment of lower pressure and lower density air, and expands further as its own density equalises with its new surroundings. This progressive expansion actually cools the air. If the rising air is warmer and lighter than its new environment, it will continue to rise until it meets an environment at the same temperature and density as itself.

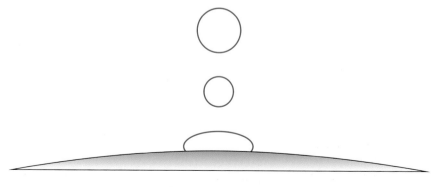

FIGURE 1.3 CONVECTION

This convection spreads heat upwards through the troposphere (where all the weather affecting light aircraft occurs), but the expansion and cooling means the average air temperature reduces progressively with height above the surface up to a certain level called the 'tropopause'. Above that is the 'stratosphere', where temperature is virtually constant.

1.8   Circulation

Air expands and rises because its density is less than that of its environment. By rising, it pushes some of the air above it outwards to make space. At the surface, some of the surrounding air flows in to fill the space from which it has risen, and is replaced by the air above it which is being pushed down by the air flowing outwards at the top. This circulation may be a local effect, but it can be also be seen over very large areas of the earth.

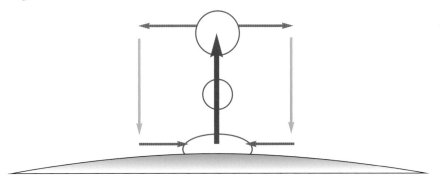

FIGURE 1.4 VERTICAL CIRCULATION

1.9   Surface Pressure

The circulation simplified in figure 1.4 does not happen instantly. The air pushed outwards at the top increases the amount of gas at the sides and reduces the amount in the middle. That means there is greater pressure of gas pushing downwards on the surface around the circulation than in the middle. In fact, any existing pressure differences will generate a similar flow.

Because similar circulations happen over large areas, we find large areas of comparatively higher and lower air pressure at the earth's surface, which can be measured and mapped. Areas of high pressure, where the air is generally descending, are called 'anticyclones'. Areas of low pressure, where the air is generally rising, are generally called 'depressions', although intense depressions have special names such as cyclones, typhoons, or hurricanes.

We can measure this 'barometric pressure' in 'bars' (one bar was the equivalent of an average surface pressure). To make exact measurements easier, the 'millibar (mb)' or one thousandth of a bar, was actually used. However, the 'Pascal' is the unit used for pressure measurement in standard metric units, and one 'hectoPascal (hPa)' (one hundred Pascals) is exactly the same as one millibar. The units tend to be used interchangeably.

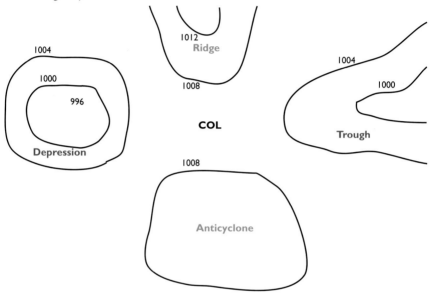

FIGURE 1.5 PRESSURE PATTERNS

The surface pressure map at figure 1.5 shows lines joining points of the same atmospheric pressure as measured or corrected for sea level. These lines, called 'isobars', are shown at intervals of 4 hectoPascals. Also marked are the names for common pressure features. Anticyclones and depressions have been described. A "tongue" of high or low pressure on the map is called a 'ridge' of high pressure or a 'trough' of low pressure. An area between two areas of high pressure and two areas of low pressure is called a 'col'.

In general terms, the mass of air above the map in figure 1.5 would be tending to move slowly downwards over the anticyclone and the ridge, and slowly upwards from the depression and trough. However, as we shall see later, such general tendency may be overtaken by local events.

6

1.10 Pressure at Height

As an aircraft climbs, there is less air above it, so the air pressure reduces, by approximately one hectoPascal per 30 feet when near sea level but progressively less at height. Barometric altimeters show altitude by measuring that pressure, comparing it with the "standard pressure setting" of 1013.2 hPa, and indicating the 'pressure altitude'. The altimeter can be corrected to other datums. For example it can indicate true altitude above sea level by setting its sub-scale to the actual sea level pressure "QNH", or height above an aerodrome by setting "QFE" (aerodrome pressure).

However, if the altimeter sub-scale is not set correctly, there will be a "barometric error". It will read more or less than the true figure. If set too high (perhaps originally in an area of higher pressure), the altimeter will read more than true (over-read), and the pilot may believe himself higher than he is, by 30 feet for every hectoPascal of difference. When flying from high pressure to low, this potentially dangerously over-reading situation can be remembered by expressions like "high - low - high", or "high to low, look out below!"

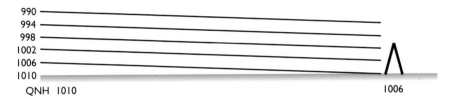

FIGURE 1.6 ALTIMETER BAROMETRIC ERROR

In figure 1.6, if the altimeter is set to a QNH of 1010, and the aircraft flies towards a lower surface pressure of 1006, the aircraft will progressively descend in true terms although the altimeter tells the pilot he is flying level. He may think he will clear the 300 foot obstruction ahead by flying at an indicated 400 feet, but the actual descent (4 hPa at 30 feet/hPa = 120 ft) will cause him to hit it.

Drawing a similar picture to fig 1.6, we could if we wished calculate an aircraft's altitude from its pressure altitude if we know the QNH.

1.11 Temperature

We do not normally measure the actual heat energy contained in an object. We do measure its surface temperature, which in practical terms is the effect its heat energy has on its surroundings. For example, a normal thermometer measures how much a fixed mass of mercury expands when affected by the heat conducted from the surface. We use the Celsius, or 'centigrade', scale to measure most aviation temperatures. The temperature at which liquid water freezes to ice is defined as zero degrees Celsius (0°C), and the temperature at which water boils (converts directly to gas) is 100°C.

Certain, usually American, instruments refer to the Fahrenheit temperature scale, in which water freezes at 32 degrees and boils at 212 degrees.

1. The earth's atmosphere is composed of gases. Which is the most common?

    a.   Oxygen
    b.   Nitrogen
    c.   Helium
    d.   Carbon dioxide

2. What is water vapour?

    a.   A gas which forms a large proportion of the earth's atmosphere
    b.   A liquid which is suspended in the earth's atmosphere
    c.   A gas which forms a small part of the earth's atmosphere
    d.   A liquid which falls as rain

3. If there is no cloud cover, at what time of day is the earth likely to be coldest?

    a.   Dawn
    b.   Shortly after dawn
    c.   Midnight
    d.   Shortly after midnight

4. If there is no cloud cover, at what time of day is the sun's heating greatest?

    a.   Shortly after dawn
    b.   Midday
    c.   One to two hours after midday
    d.   Shortly before sunset

5. What does 'diurnal' mean?

    a.   Varying between hot and cold
    b.   Varying with the time of year
    c.   Varying between day and night
    d.   Varying with time throughout a 24 hour period

6. Where does most of the earth's weather occur?

    a.   In the tropopause
    b.   In the stratosphere
    c.   In the troposphere
    d.   In the isobar

7. What is an anticyclone?

    a.   An area of low surface atmospheric pressure
    b.   A line joining places of equal surface pressure
    c.   An area above which a mass of air is slowly sinking
    d.   A shelter against tropical storms

8. In the absence of cloud cover, at what time of day is the earth at its warmest?

    a.   Midday
    b.   About 2 hours after midday
    c.   Just before sunset
    d.   Just after sunset

9. Why do diurnal variations occur?

    a.   Because the earth travels round the sun
    b.   Because the earth is tilted at about 23°
    c.   Because the earth is a spheroid
    d.   Because the earth spins on its axis

10. Which of the following surfaces is likely to reflect the sun's energy most?

    a.   Dark earth
    b.   Cloud
    c.   Snow
    d.   A forest

11. If cloud forms overnight and remains all day, what effect would you expect that to have on the temperature at the surface, compared with an area without cloud?

    a.   It will be colder at dawn, but warmer in the afternoon
    b.   It will be colder at dawn, and colder in the afternoon
    c.   It will be warmer at dawn, but colder in the afternoon
    d.   It will be warmer at dawn , and warmer in the afternoon

12. What is the correct name for a line joining places with equal atmospheric pressure?

    a.   An anticyclone
    b.   An isogonal
    c.   An isobar
    d.   An isopascal

13. Above which of these features would you most likely find the air mass to be slowly rising?

    a.   A ridge
    b.   A trough
    c.   A col
    d.   A pole

Intentionally Left Blank

Chapter 2

Water

2.1 Introduction

Water exists on the earth in various forms. As a liquid, it is found in the oceans, lakes and rivers which cover ⅔ of the earth's surface, and is also visible as the liquid drops which form cloud. As a solid, ice, it is found where heating is insufficient to melt it; around the poles, on high mountains, and as crystals in high clouds. As a gas, water vapour exists in the atmosphere in small amounts. However, that small amount has a great influence on our weather.

2.2 Water Vapour

Although we think of water turning from liquid to gas when it 'boils' (at 100°C), a certain amount of any liquid will 'evaporate' into vapour at lower temperatures when it comes into contact with a gas which is prepared to absorb it. Water will evaporate from the surface of a lake or ocean into the air above.

The amount of water vapour which a mass of air can absorb depends on the temperature of that air. At high temperatures, a lot of water vapour can be absorbed; at low temperatures, the air can "hold" much less water vapour. We talk about the 'relative humidity' of a mass of air, and measure it as the amount of water vapour in that air compared to the amount it could hold at its current temperature. This proportion is measured as a percentage, for example "50% humidity".

2.3 Condensation

If air which has absorbed a certain amount of water vapour is cooled down, its humidity will increase as its temperature drops (although it is holding the same amount of water vapour, the amount it can hold is less than before). At some stage, relative humidity will become 100%. At this point the air is holding as much water vapour as it can, we say the air is 'saturated'.

If the air cools below this temperature, known as the 'dew point', some of the vapour has to turn back into water drops. This is 'condensation'. The drops formed are usually very small and light, and so may stay suspended in the air for some time, although one would expect gravity to bring them down to earth. The steam we see from a boiling kettle is actually a cloud of these condensed droplets, formed when the hot saturated vapour is cooled below its dew point as it mixes with the colder air outside the kettle.

Dew forms on a summer's morning when moist air is cooled by radiation overnight and the condensed water droplets fall to the ground. We see these on blades of grass, for example. However, if another force were present to push the drops upwards against gravity, they would not descend, and a group of these condensed droplets would form a layer of fog, called 'radiation fog'. If dust particles are also present, the water droplets tend to cluster around these, forming larger drops.

FIGURE 2.1 RADIATION FOG DEVELOPING

2.4   Turbulence Clouds

The force which 'lifts' the water droplets to oppose gravity in our example of radiation fog above is turbulence. This force is produced when a wind (generated by air attempting to flow from high pressure to low) meets some vertical obstruction such as a building, a clump of trees or even some blades of grass, and is pushed upwards to pass over the obstruction. As the air is pushed upwards, it lifts the water droplets and prevents them dropping to earth. By remaining suspended in the air, the droplets reduce visibility and reflect the sun's heat.

A wind of as little as 2 knots (nautical miles per hour) is enough to form radiation fog. An increase in wind strength produces an increase in the height of the top of the fog layer, making it thicker. However, if the wind becomes stronger than about 8 knots, the turbulence becomes strong enough to produce enough eddies in the atmosphere to allow the air to contract as it descends and warm up again. Having warmed up, it can absorb some of the water back into vapour. This produces a relatively clear layer below the layer of water droplets, which as 'cloud' extends from a certain height above the ground to another height.

Because this cloud is in the form of a layer, we use a Latin name for "layer" to describe it, and call it 'stratus' cloud. If the wind is even stronger, the 'base' or bottom of the cloud rises, the turbulent eddies become more pronounced, the cloud becomes thicker, and the top of the layer takes on a "heaped" appearance. The Latin name for "heap" is 'cumulus' so we call this "heaped layer" cloud 'stratocumulus'.

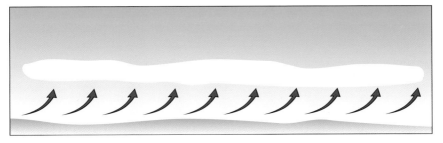

FIGURE 2.2 STRATUS CLOUD

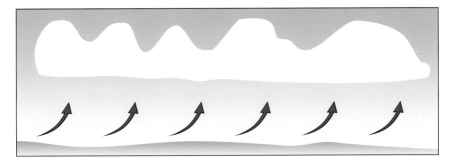

FIGURE 2.3 STRATOCUMULUS CLOUD

2.5 Hill Fog

Where there is a slope in the ground, wind may push the air upwards. As the pushed air rises, it mixes with air of lower density and pressure, expands and cools. If the air is moist (if the humidity is high) that cooling may bring the air below its dew point and stratus cloud may form. If the cloud actually touches the ground, we call it 'hill fog'.

As the air in contact with the ground is pushed uphill, the air above that is also forced to rise. Even if the air in contact with the ground does not become saturated itself, some of that higher air may reach its dew point. If that happens, stratus or stratocumulus cloud will form at a higher level.

It can be seen that if the 'air mass' is moist, cloud is likely on or above any 'windward' slopes. During pre-flight planning, pilots should avoid such areas if humidity is high, and should be prepared for such 'orographic' (associated with hills) cloud to form. Each part of the cloud which forms drifts with the wind, and is replaced by another. Pilots often fail to notice that, as they also drift with the wind believing that they are in clear air, the next patch of orographic cloud is forming on or above the windward side of the slope, around them.

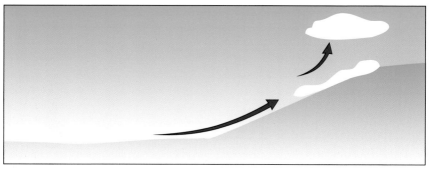

FIGURE 2.4 OROGRAPHIC CLOUD

FIGURE 2.5 HILL FOG

16

2.6   Convective Cloud

In chapter 1 we met the convective process. As the sun heats the earth, some areas on the surface become warmer than others, and the air above them also becomes warmer by conduction. That warmer air expands, becomes less dense (lighter) and starts to rise. As it rises, it expands further, and that expansion cools it. If the rising air is still warmer than the environment (surroundings) which it has reached, it will continue to rise. If the continued rising, expansion, and 'adiabatic' (which refers to this type of cooling by expansion) cooling eventually brings the temperature of the rising air below its dew point, little heaps of 'cumulus' cloud will form. The pockets of rising air (thermals) often form themselves into columns starting from the hot area of the surface, which produces thicker and longer lasting cumulus clouds.

While the rising and expanding air is above its dew point, this adiabatic cooling reduces its temperature by 3 degrees Celsius for every thousand feet the air has risen. This rate of 3°C per thousand feet is called the 'dry adiabatic lapse rate', often shortened to 'DALR'. Meteorologists use this rate to calculate how far a pocket of air is expected to rise. They measure the temperature profile (amongst other things) of the environment air mass by sending up radio balloons equipped with sophisticated instruments. Having decided what temperature can be expected at the surface, they can calculate what temperature a rising pocket of air will be at any altitude. By comparing the calculated temperature of any potential rising air pocket with the measured temperature of the environment air mass, they can calculate the maximum altitude which any convective circulation (with its resulting turbulence) will reach.

FIGURE 2.6 CUMULUS

2.7   Cloud Base

The dew point of rising air will also reduce (by half a degree for every thousand feet), so a meteorologist (or a pilot with the necessary information) could calculate the altitude of the cloudbase, if convection goes that high. Having worked out the top of the convective layer as in the paragraph above, all he has to do is take the temperature and dew point at the surface, and divide the difference by 2½ to find the potential cloudbase in thousands of feet. For example, if the surface temperature is 15°C and the dew point is 10°C, the cloudbase will be (15-10 =) 5/2½ = 2,000 feet if convection goes that high. The same result is achieved if we multiply the difference by 4 to find the cloudbase in hundreds of feet (5 x 4 = 20).

2.8   Cloud Depth

Once rising air reaches its dew point and cloud forms, the now 'saturated' air continues to rise and cool, and water drops continue to condense out. However, the process of changing state from gas to liquid actually warms the air slightly (we say it releases the "latent heat of vaporisation"), so the overall rate of cooling is reduced as it continues to rise. At low altitudes, that rate of cooling of the saturated air is halved, and the 'saturated adiabatic lapse rate (SALR)' is approximately 1.5°C per thousand feet. (Because the rising air holds less water at lower temperatures, at high altitudes there is progressively less warming, so the SALR increases with height.)

Having found the height of cloudbase, we could if we wished use the SALR to re-calculate how much higher the rising air will climb. Complex Graphs from the balloon soundings, called 'tephigrams (T- grams)', are available for those (such as glider pilots) who may wish to study and draw their own conclusions from the convective structure of the atmosphere. The rest of us shall assume that the forecaster has interpreted them correctly.

As can be seen in the information extracted from a tephigram and plotted in simplified form in figure 2.7, in a particular mass of air the temperature variations with pressure altitude can be quite extreme, and are often far from smooth. However, the average 'environmental lapse rate' or 'ELR' from the earth's surface to the tropopause works out at about 2 degrees Celsius per thousand feet.

The temperatures in figure 2.7 have been plotted every 1000 feet of pressure altitude. Although in general the temperature decreases with altitude (at an average of 1.5°C per thousand feet), we can see that between 6000 and 7000 feet the environmental temperature actually increases. We call this increase in temperature with height an 'inversion'. Between 2000 and 3000 feet the temperature appears to remain constant, and this is called an 'isothermal layer'.

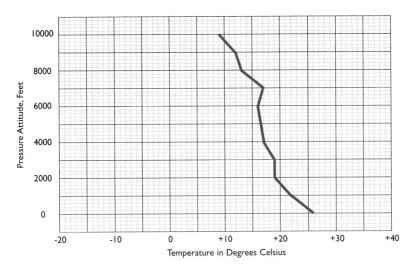

FIGURE 2.7 TEMPERATURE CHANGE WITH HEIGHT

In figure 2.8, we see what would happen to dry air which started with the environment at 26°C at sea level and was given a slight nudge upwards (by convection, orographic or other form of lifting). As it rises above the surface, it cools adiabatically, but is still warmer than its environment, so it continues rising, shown as the blue line. Because of this, we say that the air is 'unstable'. If the rising, cooling, air had risen into an environment which was warmer than itself, it would have tried to descend again, and we would have called it 'stable'.

In figure 2.8, at 2200 feet, the rising, previously unstable, air (in blue) would meet environmental air at the same temperature as itself, and would stop rising If the dew point at that point was lower than +19°C, no cloud would form. However, if by chance the air became saturated at 1000 feet, the rising air would follow the green SALR line upwards from there. No longer would it stop at 2200 feet. Because it would now be cooling at 1.5°C per thousand feet, the air would continue to rise until it reached an environment with an equal temperature at 4,900 feet. Cloud would form with its base at 1000 feet, and the top at that 4,900 feet.

A meteorologist would describe air with characteristics similar to that between 3000 feet and 4000 feet in figures 2.7 and 2.8 (where the lapse rate is less than 3° but more than 1.5° per thousand feet and the graph slopes less than the DALR and more than the SALR) as "conditionally unstable" because it would be stable when dry but unstable if it were saturated.

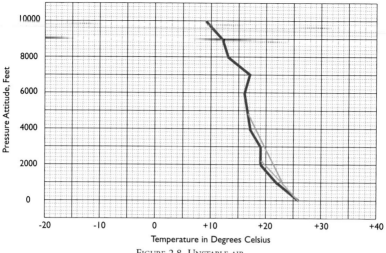

FIGURE 2.8 UNSTABLE AIR

2.9 Fronts

So far, we have considered a mass of air with generally common characteristics. The circulations mentioned in chapter 1 may take place on a large scale. For example, in summer a continent will heat up more than its surrounding ocean, generating a large circulation centred over itself. In winter, a continent, especially one near the pole, will lose heat by radiation and become an area of high pressure (anticyclone) which "blocks" the movement of the low pressure circulations which tend to flow round it. These long lasting circulations retain a mass of air in one place for a long time, so each 'air mass' takes on specific characteristics from its place of origin.

If some of that air mass does move, as it eventually does, these original characteristics become affected by the surface over which it travels. For example, a dry warm air mass will absorb water vapour from an ocean as it travels over it, although its dew point is likely to be changed least by its travels. Warm or cold ocean currents will affect air masses differently.

Depressions, the heart of large scale circulations, attract air masses from different origins or paths, and when different air masses meet there is usually considerable activity at the boundary. Fluids (liquids and gases) do not mix easily (think about hot and cold water running into a bath from taps at opposite ends; you have to physically mix them or you end up with a hot end and a cold end). The boundaries between air masses are marked by 'fronts', and at these fronts the interaction between the air masses produces vertical movement, sometimes on a vast scale.

If a generally warmer air mass is pushed (see the next chapter on "wind") into a generally colder one, we call the boundary a 'warm front'. The warmer air, being less dense, rises over the colder air, and as it rises it expands and cools adiabatically all along the front. The 'frontal surface' develops into a huge slope, represented in figure 2.9, up which the warmer air is pushed (typically about 1 in 150 or 300 feet per mile), and if the warmer air is also moist (as it usually is when it reaches the UK, having collected water vapour during an ocean passage) then cloud will form at many altitudes up to the tropopause. The formation and movement of this frontal cloud is often quite erratic, and many pilots have been surprised by apparent clear areas suddenly 'filling in'.

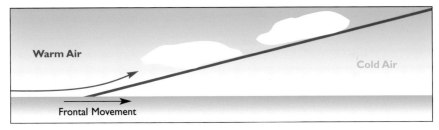

FIGURE 2.9 WARM FRONT

A colder air mass pushing up against a warmer air mass is called a 'cold front'. In this case the warmer air is physically pushed upwards out of the way of the advancing cold air, so a cold front tends to produce deep convective cloud, and the boundary between the two air masses has a steeper slope (typically about 1 in 50 or 100 feet per mile).

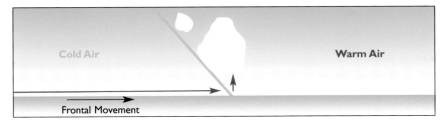

FIGURE 2.10 COLD FRONT

A cold front moves across the surface faster than a warm front, so tends to catch up with it. Where it does, a complicated set of boundaries appear, which we call an 'occluded front' or 'occlusion'. Here a wedge of warm air is being pushed upwards and away from the depression at high level, and the type of cloud formed depends on the relative characteristics of the three air masses. The one pictured in figure 2.11 is a 'cold' occlusion, where the air behind the warm air is colder than the air in front of it.

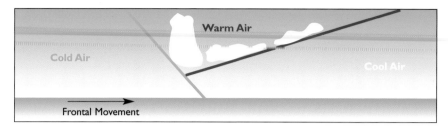

FIGURE 2.11 OCCLUDED FRONT

2.10 Air Masses over the UK

The air masses which commonly affect the UK are given names by meteorologists. A "tropical" air mass has started from somewhere warmer than the UK, as against a "polar" air mass from a colder area, or an "arctic" one from the actual polar region itself. The masses are also described by their relative humidity, either "maritime" with a high humidity or "continental" with a lower humidity.

An air mass starting over Canada (the source of the UK's "polar maritime" air) may initially drift South over the Atlantic but then turn back Northwards again. As it crosses progressively cooler water its humidity increases, and it is then referred to as "returning polar maritime". It has similar characteristics to the "tropical maritime" air which normally starts over the Atlantic near the Azores. "Polar continental" comes from Siberia, and "tropical continental" comes from North Africa, while "Arctic maritime" comes directly from the polar ice cap.

The classic sequence of air masses around a depression crossing the UK is for returning polar maritime air to be followed at a warm front by tropical maritime air. That in turn is pushed up by polar maritime air at the following cold front, until the cold front catches up with the warm front and forms a cold occlusion. The warm air is progressively 'squeezed' upwards and outwards from the depression. However, this is by no means the only system which pilots will meet.

2.11 Ice Clouds

Cloud at a warm front is basically stratus. At very high altitudes the temperatures are so low that when the water vapour condenses, it freezes into ice crystals. Often the first indication to a watcher on the surface of a warm front approaching is a patch of white wispy clouds called 'cirrus', because it looks like strands of hair. Similar cloud is seen formed when water vapour from aircraft engines condenses behind it at high altitude in 'condensation trails'.

FIGURE 2.12 Cirrus and cirrostratus above cumulus

In fact, the word 'cirrus' is used to describe ice crystal cloud, so when the ice cloud becomes thicker and covers the sky in a sheet, we call it 'cirrostratus'. A cumulus type cloud at very high altitude can be described as 'cirrocumulus', but is not often seen in the UK.

2.12   High Altitude Water Cloud

At altitudes below cirrus cloud, the temperature is still below freezing. However, unless the temperature is really cold (-30°C or so) it is a fact that most of the condensed vapour remains as water droplets. We distinguish the clouds which form at high altitudes (above about 8000 feet in the UK but below cirrus levels) by putting 'alto' in front of the other descriptive name. Cumulus with a base above 8000 feet would be called 'altocumulus' and stratus with a similar base would be called 'altostratus'.

2.13   Rain Cloud

The water droplets which form cloud often cluster together to form larger drops, especially around dust particles. When these larger drops descend, they take longer to evaporate than small droplets, so if the base of the cloud in which they form is low, they will not completely evaporate before they reach the ground. This 'drizzle' is often associated with low stratus cloud.

However, if the force opposing gravity is strong, some water drops become quite large. If they are carried up to where the temperature of the air and the dust particles is below freezing, some may freeze into ice pellets or 'hail', especially if the dust particles are large. When these ice pellets descend, it takes a long time for the ice to melt to water, and after that there is little time for the melted drops to evaporate, so 'rain' reaches the ground. If the pellets do not melt, hail reaches the surface. If ice crystals reach the ground in temperate latitudes, that is 'snow'.

Cloud which is thick enough to produce rain reduces the amount of sunlight passing through it, and appears dark and threatening. A Latin name given to such rain-bearing clouds is "nimbus". So thick cloud out of which it appears that 'precipitation' (a word which includes rain, hail, and snow) may reach the ground, has "nimbus" in its name. Thick stratus type cloud is called 'nimbostratus', and deep cumulus can be called 'cumulonimbus', although that name tends to be kept for the largest cumulus which produce not only precipitation but storms. Showers of rain or snow may fall from ordinary cumulus, as in figure 2.13.

FIGURE 2.13 RAIN SHOWER FROM CUMULUS

2.14 Cloud Reporting

The amount of cloud is measured as an observer sees it covering the sky. It may be measured in eighths or 'oktas'. For example, fair weather cumulus may produce 3/8 cover, while stratus may cover 8/8. This measurement can mislead pilots, as 4/8 cumulus (half cover) often leaves only small gaps between the clouds through which an aircraft can climb or descend while remaining clear of them.

For more general reporting purposes, other expressions are used to describe the cloud amounts.

- "Overcast" means complete cover of cloud, or 8 oktas.
- "Broken" means between 5 and 7 oktas, or more than half the sky is covered.
- "Scattered" means between 3 and 4 oktas, which is half cover or a little less.
- "Few" means one or 2 oktas.
- "Sky clear" may be used to describe a sky with no cloud at all.

FIGURE 2.14 SCATTERED CLOUD

Intentionally Left Blank

1. Water vapour is a ...

   a. colourless liquid?
   b. colourless gas?
   c. white solid?
   d. visible cloud of steam?

2. When water vapour changes state to liquid drops;

   a. Heat is given off
   b. Heat is absorbed
   c. No heat change takes place
   d. It cannot change state

3. Cloud formed by mechanical turbulence effects is normally referred to as ...

   a. Cumulus type?
   b. Stratus type?
   c. Nimbus type?
   d. Cirrus type?

4. Cloud from which rain may be expected to fall is normally referred to as ...

   a. Cumulus type?
   b. Stratus type?
   c. Nimbus type?
   d. Orographic type?

5. Cloud formed by air rising over hills is normally referred to as ...

   a. Cumulus type?
   b. Orographic type?
   c. Nimbus type?
   d. Cirrus type?

6. Cloud formed as a result of convection is normally referred to as ...

    a.   Cumulus type?
    b.   Stratus type?
    c.   Orographic type?
    d.   Cirrus type?

7. If the surface temperature is +20°C , and the surface dew point is +10°C, at what height would you expect cumulus cloud to form if the air is unstable?

    a.   1000 feet agl
    b.   3000 feet agl
    c.   4000 feet agl
    d.   10,000 feet agl

8. If the temperature at the surface is +20°C, and the temperature 1000 feet above the surface is +16°C, would you expect the air to be ...

    a.   Stable?
    b.   Conditionally unstable?
    c.   Unstable?
    d.   Saturated?

9. If the temperature at 1000 feet is +22°C and the temperature at 2000 feet is +20°C, would you expect the air between those altitudes to be ...

    a.   Stable?
    b.   Conditionally unstable?
    c.   Unstable?
    d.   Saturated?

10. If the temperature at 1000 feet is +20°C and the temperature at 2000 feet is +21°C, we call the layer between these two altitudes ...

    a.   An isothermal layer?
    b.   Unstable?
    c.   A tropopause?
    d.   An inversion?

11. Which is the most common type of cloud normally found at a warm front?

    a.   Stratus type cloud
    b.   Cumulus type cloud
    c.   Orographic type cloud
    d.   No cloud would be expected

12. What do we call the place where a cold airmass catches up with and pushes a warm air mass upwards?

    a.   A col
    b.   A ridge
    c.   A cold front
    d.   A warm front

13. An air mass which originates over the North American continent in winter and crosses the Atlantic Ocean towards the UK can be expected to ...

    a.   Cool down as it crosses the ocean
    b.   Absorb water droplets from the cold ocean
    c.   Lose water vapour as it crosses the ocean
    d.   Increase its humidity from the warmer ocean

14. The sky is covered in cloud. How many 'oktas' would be reported?

    a.   1
    b.   4
    c.   8
    d.   10

15. The sky is almost but not completely covered in cloud. What word would be used to describe the cloud?

    a.   Overcast
    b.   Broken
    c.   Scattered
    d.   Few

Intentionally Left Blank

Chapter 3

Wind

3.1 Introduction

The pressure variations at the surface of the earth described in chapter 1 produce a flow of air across that surface in an attempt to equalise that pressure. The greater the difference of pressure over a certain distance, or the shorter the distance between two points of a certain pressure difference (the "pressure gradient"), the greater the force trying to achieve that equalisation. This is the "pressure gradient force".

The actual pressure gradient can be found by looking at a surface pressure chart, similar to that at figures 1.5 or 3.5, and measuring the pressure difference (in hectoPascals) per hundred nautical miles. Pilots, who do not need exact measurements, can deduce approximately what they need.

3.2 Geostrophic Force

Because the earth is spinning around its axis and rotating around the sun, any object on the earth is also rotating. If however that object is free to move in relation to the spinning earth, its rotation relative to space starts to take effect. A mass of air being influenced by a pressure gradient force will actually travel in a different path to the earth under it.

As observers on the earth's surface, we see the air gradually turning to one side relative to us as it moves. In the Northern hemisphere, the air tends to turn right, and to the left in the Southern hemisphere. It appears to us that some force is turning the moving air, and we call this apparent force the 'coriolis' or 'geostrophic' force.

Detailed explanations can be found in other books, but for our purposes all we need to know is that at a particular place the strength of this coriolis or geostrophic force increases with the speed at which the air is moving.

3.3　The Balance of Forces

Air is encouraged to move by the pressure gradient force. As soon as it moves, it is affected by a small amount of geostrophic force, which in the Northern hemisphere tends to turn it to the right. As it accelerates, the geostrophic force increases and continues to turn it to the right until the two forces, pressure gradient and geostrophic, are balanced. This happens when the air is actually moving at 90° to the pressure gradient, in other words along the isobars. The speed at which the air moves is governed by the pressure gradient (as seen by the distance between the isobars on a chart), but the faster it moves the greater the geostrophic force.

Unless some other force becomes involved, the two forces balance at all times, as at the end of the arrow in the simplified picture in figure 3.1. This means that the wind flows along the isobars, at a speed depending (inversely) on the distance between these isobars (tight isobars - high winds), with the low pressure on its left in the Northern Hemisphere (low pressure on its right in the Southern Hemisphere). The direction is always measured as that from which the wind is coming. If North is at the top of the page in figure 3.1 the 'geostrophic' wind direction is 270°.

This flow parallel with the isobars and at 90° to the pressure gradient suggests that the pressure will never change. However, other factors become involved, as we shall see later, so slow changes do take place.

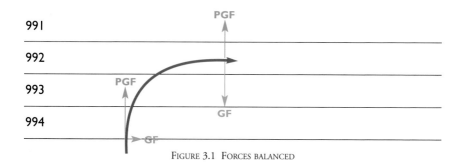

FIGURE 3.1 FORCES BALANCED

3.4　The Gradient Wind

If the isobars on the chart are straight, the strength of the geostrophic wind is proportional to the pressure gradient. However, in almost every practical case the isobars are curved. For the wind to continue to follow the isobars, as it does, there must be an imbalance between the two forces. Pressure gradient force cannot change, so the geostrophic force must; in other words the wind speed must change.

Around a depression, the 'gradient wind' is less than the pressure gradient would suggest. Around an anticyclone, the gradient wind is stronger. This gradient wind is the actual wind which we find at about 2-3000 feet above the earth's surface. For navigation purposes, as in figure 3.2, wind is often marked as a triple arrow, with its length in proportion to the wind speed.

FIGURE 3.2 GRADIENT WIND AROUND A DEPRESSION

3.5   Friction and the Surface Wind

In chapter 2 we saw the effect of turbulence on the air's vertical motion. This turbulence produced by the wind hitting obstacles on the earth's surface takes energy away from the wind, and slows the air's horizontal motion. This means that as we get closer to the surface from the level of the gradient wind, the wind strength progressively reduces.

As the wind speed reduces close to the surface, the geostrophic force also reduces, so the wind at the surface (or at 3 metres above it which is the official height at which the 'surface wind' is measured) is not only less strong, but its direction is altered towards the low pressure.

In the northern hemisphere the wind at the surface points to the left of the gradient wind. We say it is 'backed' or turned anticlockwise. The gradient wind points to the right of the surface wind; we say it is 'veered' or turned clockwise. The overall effect of the friction (in the northern hemisphere) is that as height increases from the surface, the actual wind experienced increases in strength and its direction veers. The more height the more strength and the more degrees! Similarly as we approach the surface from the height at which the gradient wind is blowing the less height the less strength and the less degrees.

FIGURE 3.3 WIND VARIATION WITH HEIGHT ABOVE THE SURFACE

The actual variation depends on several factors. For example at night the surface wind is very light (perhaps 20% of the gradient wind) and the friction effect is felt over only about the bottom 500 feet, so the change is very marked over that 'friction layer'. During the day, the added heat from the sun mixes the friction through a much deeper layer, and on a summer's day the surface wind may be about 2/3 of the gradient wind and the layer may be almost 3000 feet thick.

A sea surface produces little friction, as would a snow field or flat grassland. Again the friction is felt over a shallow layer, the wind at the surface is very light, but the wind shear (the change in wind strength with height from the surface, which can cause airspeed problems on the approach) is severe. Buildings in a city, however, or a rocky landscape, can be expected to produce a great deal of friction. Greater friction does not produce a greater reduction in surface wind; in fact the greater the friction, the more the reduced surface wind mixes with the gradient wind, the less the wind shear, and the closer the mean surface wind is to the gradient wind in strength and direction.

3.6   Thermal Winds

As we have seen in chapter 2, different air masses have different characteristics, amongst which are their temperatures. Warm air is less dense than cold air, so even if the pressure at the surface is the same, the pressure at height will be different. Pressure is the weight of air above a unit area (the weight of a column of air of unit cross section). The pressure at a certain height (for example 3000 feet above the ground) is the weight of the total column less the weight of the bottom 3000 feet. The pressure at 3000 feet in warm air will be higher than the pressure at 3000 feet in cold air because the mass of the warm air is less than the mass of the colder air, as in figure 3.4.

FIGURE 3.4 THERMAL PRESSURE DIFFERENCES

If there were no variations in surface pressure, there would be no pressure gradient, and no gradient wind. However, at height (3000 feet in figure 3.4) there would indeed be a pressure gradient, so a tendency for wind to blow. This may go under the name of a "thermal wind", attempting to blow from high temperature to low temperature. Of course, once such a wind starts to blow, geostrophic force (coriolis) tends to turn it, so the practical effect is for the thermal wind to blow with the low temperature on its left in the northern hemisphere. Since there is almost invariably a surface pressure gradient and a gradient wind, the actual wind at a given height is actually a combination of this "thermal component" and the gradient wind generated by the surface pressure.

3.7   Fronts

The positions of the fronts between air masses are marked on surface pressure charts, at the points where they touch the surface. As we have seen in chapter 2, they slope considerably with height. At about 2000 feet, the wind blows along the isobars. As height increase the thermal component increases, and when close to the frontal surface near the tropopause the wind blows strongly along that frontal surface, often so strongly that we call it a 'jet stream'. Figure 3.5 shows a surface pressure chart of a depression with warm and cold fronts marked. Also marked in purple are the positions above which a jet stream (very strong upper wind) may be found, in the area of the UK at about 34,000 feet (a lot higher than any light aircraft).

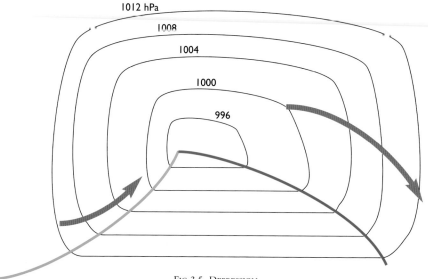

FIG 3.5 DEPRESSION

The fronts move across the earth's surface in the general direction of the gradient wind, in fact at approximately 90 degrees to the marked 'surface front'. A cold front (represented earlier at figure 2.7), where a more energetic cold air mass pushes the warmer air upwards out of its path, moves at an average speed about equal to that of the gradient wind at its position, although local fluctuations occur. A warm front, where the more sluggish warm air slides over the colder air (see figure 2.9), moves at only about 2/3 of the speed of the gradient wind in its area. Cold fronts usually catch up with warm fronts, producing occlusions (as in figure 2.11), whose speed of movement is less predictable, depending on whether the occlusion more closely resembles a warm or a cold front.

At the surface, despite the simplified drawing in figure 3.5, the wind tends to back as the front approaches. As the front passes, the surface wind veers, which is a fair indication (visible on a windsock) to an observer that the air mass has changed, although it may take some time before the general weather changes.

3.8   Gusts

The turbulence caused close to the ground by friction or convection not only causes a general increase in the expected surface wind but produces variations in that wind. These variations are what we call "gusts" (increases) and "lulls" (decreases). By their very nature, gusts are not only stronger than the average surface wind, but usually veer in direction (more knots and more degrees), while lulls tend to back.

Mechanical turbulence (friction) produces fewer and weaker gusts than thermal turbulence (convection). The maximum strength of even convective gusts is usually limited to the strength of the gradient wind. However, light aircraft have low inertia; a rapid change of wind speed and/or direction can produce a considerable airspeed change when close to the ground, especially at slow speeds such as on the approach or just after take-off.   That low inertia can also cause rapid reductions in airspeed when making an approach through a strong wind sheer.

Gusts lasting for a considerable time are called "squalls", usually associated with groups of cumulus or cumulonimbus clouds. These groups are often found along a line between colder air advancing into warmer, whether a marked cold front or a local affect, in which case they are referred to as a "line squall". Line squalls and individual cumulonimbus clouds can be expected to include gusts with strengths in excess of the gradient wind.

3.9   Thermals

So far in this chapter we have been considering the movement of large amounts of air. The same principles apply to more localised effects. "Thermals", in which birds and gliders may climb, are convective currents and affect all light aircraft. Apart from the horizontal gusts felt close to the ground, as an aircraft flies through the rising and falling air the change in the air's vertical speed can also cause airspeed fluctuations and even vary the angle at which the air strikes the aerofoil. Unless the pilot needs to stay above or below a certain altitude, he will find it convenient to allow the aircraft to change height as the thermals affect it.

As with clouds, thermals may form in 'streets' along the direction of the wind. However, they are not continuously rising columns, nor are they always topped with cumulus clouds, even when such clouds are visible. On a hot day, or when the air is unstable, pilots should expect thermals to affect their flight, and be prepared for sudden variations in the surface wind as well as vertical motion.

3.10 Sea Breeze

Clear skies in summer the diurnal variations in temperature noted in chapter 1 often produce smaller versions of the thermal wind. This is usually most obvious near the coast, because sea temperatures do not change much over a period of 24 hours, whereas land temperatures do.

During the day, the sun heats up the land, and convection can spread this heat into the air above, reducing its density and creating a similar pressure difference at the top of the convection layer to that described in paragraph 3.6. The effect is shown in figure 3.6 below. The pressure difference at about 3000 feet produces a flow at that level from the land towards the sea. Coriolis takes time to come into effect, so that flow increases the amount of air over the sea area, increasing the surface pressure and producing a pressure gradient at the surface. This in turn encourages a wind at the surface from the sea to the land, the "sea breeze".

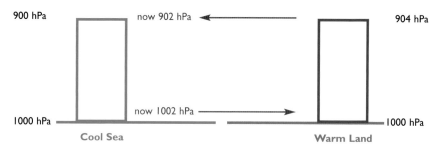

FIGURE 3.6 SEA BREEZE

The colder air from the sea cools down the land over which it blows, so the division between the two air masses moves inland during the day. When the sea breeze starts, the induced wind blows at right angles to the coast. However, as the air moves, coriolis starts to take effect, so the wind at the coast itself tends to veer (in the Northern hemisphere) as the day progresses. Figure 3.7 shows a greatly simplified version of the surface wind changing at different distances from the coastline as the day progresses.

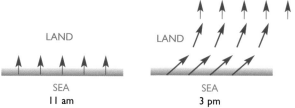

FIGURE 3.7 COASTAL WIND DIRECTIONS AT DIFFERENT TIMES OF DAY

At night, the air over the land cools down below the sea temperatures, and the effect is reversed to produce a 'land breeze' in the early hours of the morning, until the land warms up again. The actual timing of the sea breeze depends on the relative temperatures between the air over the land and the sea, which varies. However, typically on a clear summer day, the sea breeze starts about 11 am (10 am local mean time) and stops after midnight once the land has cooled down again. The land breeze, which tends to be lighter and of shorter duration because of seasonal variation, then starts and continues until mid morning.

Although the sea breeze is the most obvious version of a small scale thermal wind, and the only one regularly seen in the UK, the effect can also be seen in other places where temperature variations occur, such as a boundary between snow fields and forests.

3.11 Words and Numbers

As mentioned earlier, the wind direction is reported as that from which the wind is blowing. In all meteorological reports, that direction is measured from true North, followed by the wind speed in knots. Runway directions are given with reference to magnetic North, so pilots have to add magnetic variation to the met wind before they can calculate crosswind or headwind components for landing or take-off. However, if air traffic control (ATC) pass a surface wind to pilots on the ground or flying in the traffic pattern, that will be with reference to magnetic North.

Historically, wind strengths used to be referred to not as speeds in knots, but as numbers on the 'Beaufort Scale' invented by a British admiral of that name for maritime use. The scale is still used in shipping forecasts, and a knowledge of it may be useful if a pilot listens to these forecasts. Directions are referred to points on a compass, i.e. "south-easterly" being from that direction.

In addition to the numbers, many words used by forecasters have specific definitions, some of which are also included below as are some of the obvious visible or audible effects which an observer may experience at each reported 'force' number.

The 'force' reported is the number equivalent to the average recorded wind. Gusts can usually be expected to reach higher speeds, which may or may not be specifically reported. For example, a surface wind of 15 knots gusting to 20 knots would probably only referred to as "force 4" but a wind of 25 knots gusting to 35 knots would be referred to as "force 6, gusting gale force 8". The names may have specific definitions in other fields; for example a 'gale warning' is issued when the surface wind is expected to reach either a mean of 34 knots, or gusting to 43 knots or more.

Beaufort Scale

Force	Mean Strength	Description	Noticeable Effect
0	less than 1 knot	calm	smoke rises vertically
1	1 - 3 knot	light	smoke drifts
2	4 - 6 knots	light	wind felt on face
3	7 - 10 knots	light	
4	11 - 16 knots	moderate	raises dust and loose paper
5	17 - 21 knots	fresh	white crests form on lakes
6	22 - 27 knots	strong	noise from telephone wires
7	28 - 33 knots	strong (near gale)	walking into wind inconvenient
8	34 - 40 knots	gale	twigs broken off trees
9	41 - 47 knots	severe gale	some slates removed from roofs
10	48 - 55 knots	storm	some trees uprooted
11	56 - 63 knots	violent storm	widespread damage
12	64 kt or more	hurricane	

1. The surface wind at midday at an airfield in the centre of England in summer is 170/10 knots. What would you expect the wind to be at 2000 feet?

    a.   210/20 knots
    b.   210/05 knots
    c.   140/20 knots
    d.   140/05 knots

2. The surface wind at an aerodrome is 180/15 knots. A warm front passes. Which of the following would you expect the most likely surface wind to be after the front passes?

    a.   180/10 knots
    b.   220/10 knots
    c.   150/10 knots
    d.   150/20 knots

3. On a summer's day, with no cloud cover, which of the following would you expect the surface wind to be at midday at an aerodrome on the South coast?

    a.   010/10 knots
    b.   100/10 knots
    c.   190/10 knots
    d.   280/10 knots

4. On a summer's day, with no cloud cover, which of the following would you expect the surface wind to be at 4 pm at an aerodrome on the South coast?

    a.   040/10 knots
    b.   190/10 knots
    c.   240/10 knots
    d.   290/10 knots

5. In the UK, you are flying towards a region of low pressure at 3000 feet. How would you expect the wind to affect your aircraft?

    a.   The aircraft would experience a headwind
    b.   The aircraft would experience drift to the right
    c.   The aircraft would experience a tailwind
    d.   The aircraft would experience drift to the left

6. Your destination aerodrome is close to a reservoir, where you see white crests on the surface of the water. The surface wind forecast for the aerodrome was 330/12 kt. What can you assume from your observation?

    a.   The surface wind is probably stronger than forecast
    b.   The surface wind is probably as forecast
    c.   The surface wind is from a different direction than forecast
    d.   The surface wind is probably lighter than forecast

7. In the Northern hemisphere, the wind at 2000 feet above the surface tends to blow ...

    a.   Across the isobars, from high pressure to low?
    b.   Across the isobars, to high pressure from low?
    c.   Along the isobars, with low pressure on its right?
    d.   Along the isobars, with low pressure on its left?

8. A weather forecaster describes the surface wind as "strong". What steady strength would you expect?

    a.   35 knots
    b.   25 knots
    c.   20 knots
    d.   15 knots

Chapter 4

Mountains and Hills

4.1   Introduction

In the last two chapters we have mainly discussed the effect of the earth's surface on air flowing across it as "turbulence". However, the shape of the ground has a much greater influence on that flow than we have seen so far. Even small hills will create local changes to the general gradient flow as well as the "orographic uplift" seen in chapter 2. The larger the hills, in general the greater the effect, and in mountainous areas the gradient wind may appear almost insignificant in comparison to the flows generated by the terrain both horizontally and vertically.

FIGURE 4.1 THE ALPS

4.2   Hillside Flow

At night, the air in contact with the ground cools with it. As it cools, air at a hill top becomes denser than the air at the same altitude around it. Being denser (heavier), it will tend to flow downhill into the valley below, being replaced by that less dense air around it. This "katabatic" flow is quite pronounced in mountainous areas.

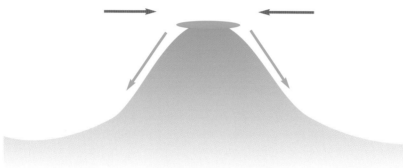

FIGURE 4.2 KATABATIC FLOW

During the day, the reverse may happen, especially if there are no clouds around. The air above the valley floor can be expected to be colder than the air below it. However, the hill top is generally heated by the sun's rays as much as the valley. After a period of heating, the air in contact with the hill top will be warmer than the air at the same altitude around it, therefore less dense (lighter) so more likely to be unstable and create convection. That convection from the hill top encourages air from the hillside to flow upwards to replace the rising air, especially (and often strongly) up slopes which are also being directly heated by the sun.

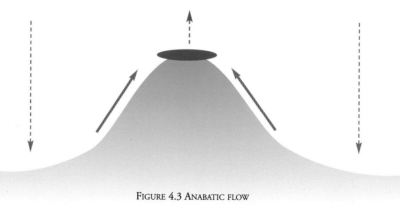

FIGURE 4.3 ANABATIC FLOW

This "anabatic" flow is often used by glider pilots, but is generally less pronounced than the katabatic flow at night. However, it is important to note that if anabatic flow is moving up a slope which is being directly heated by the sun, a slope in shadow may be influenced by what is effectively katabatic flow to replace the air in the bottom of the valley.

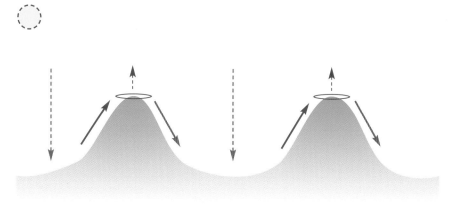

FIGURE 4.4 HILL FLOW

A combination of anabatic and katabatic flows up and down small valleys leading into a larger one often produces a local diurnal effect of a wind flowing down the main valley (perhaps quite strongly) during the night and early morning, and then changing by 180 degrees to flow up the main valley by midday. This effect is independent of the gradient wind, which in many Alpine valleys is virtually irrelevant.

4.3 Flow Over Ridges

Where the gradient wind meets a ridge or line of hills, or a range of mountains, it cannot flow through it. As seen in chapter 2, it may be pushed up over it, especially if the air is unstable. In that case, what happens next depends considerably on the stability of the air at different levels above the ground. In the majority of cases, however, the flow close to the top of the ridge will show a similar effect to that illustrated in figure 4.5. Glider pilots may be able to climb in the rising air on the windward side, but the air downwind (to the "lee") of the rising air is not only sinking but often very turbulent.

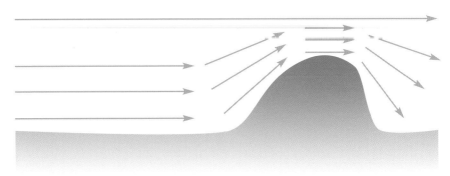

FIGURE 4.5 CROSS-RIDGE FLOW

As may be seen from the flow arrows being closer together as the air crosses the top of the ridge, the wind speed there increases above that expected from gradient calculations. Sometimes this increase may be considerable, in which case the air pressure there will also reduce (as 'Bernouli' suggests from aerodynamics). This pressure reduction is the 'hill error' in altimetry, one reason for adding 1000 feet to the elevation of the highest ground to find 'safety altitude' (the altitude below which you should not continue to fly unless you can see clearly ahead).

When the winds at increasing heights above the ground are from more or less the same direction, and where a more stable layer lies between two unstable layers, the rising air on the windward side of the ridge may not become "squeezed", but produce a corresponding rise in the air above it. This will be followed by a corresponding descent, downstream of the ridge. Where the rising air is moist, a cloud will form (see chapter 2), and as air continues to flow upwards in front of the ridge, cloud continues to form, apparently in the same place over the ground despite the strong wind. The descending air warms up and the cloud disappears, again over a particular point on the ground. Such cloud tends to take on the shape of a lens, so is frequently called "lenticular" cloud.

4.4   Wave

If the wind increases with height, the descending air downwind of the ridge may 'bounce' back upwards again, as shown in figure 4.6. This produces a smooth form of wave motion in the atmosphere which can extend for a long distance downwind (or to 'lee') of the ridge, and to great heights, even into the stratosphere. The vertical motion in this 'lee wave' may exceed a thousand feet per minute at times, and glider pilots use the rising air to make high and sometimes long flights. For the pilot of a light powered aircraft, the sinking air is the danger - if flying in the lee of the ridge, a pilot trying to climb may find his aircraft cannot do that even with full power selected. The best action may be to turn downwind until the sinking air starts to rise again, when a turn should be made back into wind.

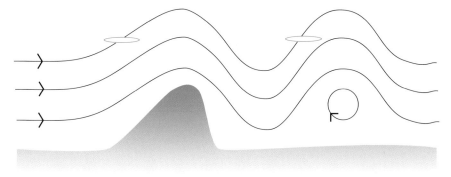

FIGURE 4.6 MOUNTAIN WAVE

Figure 4.6 also shows another effect of wave motion. At the bottom of a wave 'bounce', the "trough", the surface wind is stronger than the gradient wind. Under the wave "crest", it is lighter. If the motion at low altitudes is strong, the first 'bounce' may induce a circulation in the air below it. This "rotor" effect produces not only severe turbulence in the air, but may also produce a surface wind which is the complete reverse of the gradient wind.

The distance between wave crests depends on many factors. As atmospheric conditions change, that wavelength also changes, sometimes quite rapidly. Pilots approaching to land when wave motion exists must be prepared for sudden changes in the surface wind as well as downdrafts from the sinking air. Always be ready to divert to a landing field unaffected by any wave motion.

Figure 4.6 shows an idealised picture of wave motion with 'classic' lenticular clouds, similar to those over the Alps in figure 4.1, but which are less usual in the UK. In our country, with its generally moister air, the wave pattern is often recognisable only by gaps in a general cloud sheet produced by the descending air, as in figure 4.7, rather than lenticular cloud in the rising air. If the cloud gaps appear to stay over the same point on the ground, and seem to lie at right angles to the gradient wind direction, they are almost certainly caused by wave motion, and pilots should be prepared for the effects. For example, climbing through these gaps will be slow in the sinking air, and cloud will continue to form in patches in front of the downwind edge of the gap, possibly around the climbing aircraft.

FIGURE 4.7 WAVE GAPS

4.5   Rotor Streaming

Conditions may not always be correct for wave motion. If for example the wind decreases with height above the ridge line, the air will not flow smoothly. In fact, the whole wave motion may break down into turbulent flow which streams downwind from the ridge top. This "rotor streaming" turbulence may be extreme, and cause serious control difficulties in light aircraft, so if it is forecast it is advisable to stay away from the area. It is usually worst when flying at a similar altitude to that of the ridge top.

4.6   The Föhn effect

Moist air flowing up a slope may produce quite thick cloud, thick enough to produce drizzle or even rain drops. Once these drops fall out of the cloud, they are no longer present in the air. Above cloudbase on the windward side, the saturated air rising up the slope will cool at the SALR, and when descending on the other side will warm up, again at the SALR, until all the cloud water drops are re-absorbed. Because some of the water has fallen out of the air, there is less to be re-absorbed, so the air going down will become unsaturated at a higher altitude than before, and will then warm at the DALR from that point downwards. The air downwind of the hill will be drier and warmer than that on the windward side. A representation of this "Föhn" effect over an 8000 foot hill is illustrated in figure 4.8.

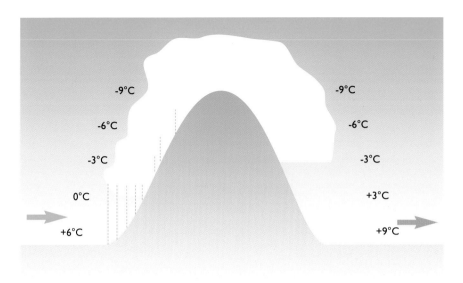

FIGURE 4.8 FÖHN EFFECT

4.7   Funnelling

Although unstable air will rise over high ground, stable air usually much prefers to take the line of least resistance, and flow round an obstruction such as a hill rather than over it. If the obstruction is a ridge or range of hills, the air will attempt to flow between the hills and along valleys. Even in unstable air, if there is a notable gradient wind and anabatic and katabatic effects are weak or non-existent (for example under cloudy skies), the wind will follow the valleys rather than climb.

This "funnel effect" through one or more valleys often increases the speed of the flow above that of the calculated gradient wind, especially as the valleys narrow and where the valley floor rises to cross a 'saddle' or pass between two hills (a similar effect to that seen at the ridge top in paragraph 4.3). Valleys through a range of hills or mountains do not lie straight, but twist and turn, and while following a line of valleys the surface wind may be flowing completely against the original gradient direction. As may be imagined, in general the narrower the valley, the stronger the wind. The flow will also be affected by 'spurs' (ridges sticking out into the valley), and turbulence downstream of these will affect the approach to any landing field in the neighbourhood.

4.8   Combinations

This chapter has given an introduction to the subject of flow and weather around hills. Although we have looked at various effects here, hills and ridges are never isolated, and the flow over and round one hill has an effect on the flow over and around the next one, and even its neighbours. Even pure wave motion from one hill will interfere with flow from another, creating more turbulence than might be expected from the flow over one hill only. To fully understand the interaction between these flows requires a considerable amount of either local knowledge or further study, much more advanced than is intended here. It is not really possible to fly safely in mountainous or even hilly terrain in anything other than clear weather and gentle wind strengths without that full understanding.

1. Which of the following most correctly describes a 'katabatic' wind?

    a.   It blows in the opposite direction to the gradient flow
    b.   It blows up a slope
    c.   It blows down a slope
    d.   It blows along a valley

2. An aerodrome is in a long steep river valley. The river flows from North to South. The gradient wind is 090/05 knots. On which runway would you expect to land in mid-afternoon?

    a.   09
    b.   18
    c.   27
    d.   36

3. If mountain wave is forecast, where would you expect to find the greatest turbulence?

    a.   Upwind of a ridge, at the height of the ridge top
    b.   Upwind of a ridge, at twice the ridge top height
    c.   Downwind of a ridge, at the height of the ridge top
    d.   Downwind of a ridge, at twice the ridge top height

4. You are flying under a sheet of continuous stratocumulus cloud. As you fly into wind towards a line of hills, gaps appear in the cloud lined up in the same direction as the hills. Which of the following effects would you be most likely to experience as you continue towards the hills?

    a.   Steady rainfall progressively increasing
    b.   Turbulence at or above the height of the hill tops
    c.   Sharp showers
    d.   A steady increase in wind strength

5. If 'lenticular 'cloud is forecast, what phenomenon would you expect?

    a.   Thunderstorms
    b.   Mountain or lee wave
    c.   Valley winds
    d.   Drizzle

6. A line of hills lies North - South. The gradient wind is moderate to strong Westerly. Hazardous conditions are most likely to be encountered when flying ...

    a.   towards the hills from the East?
    b.   towards the hills from the West?
    c.   parallel with the hills on the West side of them?
    d.   no hazardous conditions are likely in these conditions

7. Mountain wave is forecast. Your aircraft cannot climb in the sinking air. In which direction should you fly to escape the downdraft?

    a.   Into wind, towards the range of hills
    b.   Across the wind, parallel to the range of hills
    c.   Down wind, away from the range of hills
    d.   The direction is irrelevant

8. What hazards are likely when flying in the lee of a range of hills?

    a.   Sinking air, turbulence and rain
    b.   Sinking air, turbulence and surface wind reversals
    c.   Sinking air, rain and surface wind reversals
    d.   Turbulence, rain, and surface wind reversals

Chapter 5

Thunderstorms

5.1 Introduction

Convective clouds are usually a sign of pleasant weather, but if carried to extremes, as 'cumulonimbus' clouds, 'cunim', or 'Cb' they become far from pleasant, and particularly hazardous to light aviation. This chapter looks at these cumulonimbus clouds, also commonly referred to as thunderstorms.

A cumulonimbus cloud is actually a combination of several smaller clouds, or 'cells'. Although we shall start by describing the development of individual cells, many of the hazards are produced by the interaction between cells at different stages of development. Some of that interaction, the electrical activity, is what defines a cumulonimbus cloud.

5.2 Requirements

For a cumulus cloud to grow into a cumulonimbus, three factors must combine. There has to be considerable moisture content in the air. The air must be unstable over a great depth, or at least 'conditionally unstable' (unstable when saturated), so that any upcurrents which develop in the moist air can continue up to the tropopause. There must also be some form of 'trigger' to start the convection going.

Meteorologists use the various types of trigger to categorise thunderstorms. A cumulonimbus cloud triggered by a cold front or an occlusion is referred to as a 'frontal thunderstorm', one triggered by air flowing up a slope is referred to as an 'orographic thunderstorm', and one triggered by thermal convection is referred to as an 'airmass thunderstorm'. Since there are major hazards in and near cumulonimbus clouds, flight in the area of any form of trigger should be avoided if the factors of instability and high moisture content are present (in which case a forecast will include the words "thunderstorm" or "cumulonimbus").

5.3   The Cumulus Stage

Each cumulonimbus cell starts as a cumulus cloud. Whatever trigger starts the air rising, as that rising air cools to saturation and forms cloud, it tends to accelerate upwards, which may overcome a shallow stable layer or even possibly an inversion. As the air continues to rise and form cloud, all the air inside that cloud is rising. At this stage, the descending air forming the classic circulation pattern shown in chapter 2 lies outside the cloud. At the surface, air is drawn in to the developing cell, either adding to or reducing the gradient wind.

Once the air has risen above the 'freezing level' (the pressure altitude above which the air temperature is below freezing), water drops which have formed around any dust particles caught in the updraft will freeze into hail. Because the updrafts are strong, the frozen drops continue to travel upwards, growing as they do. As mentioned earlier, despite temperatures below freezing, many of the drops do not freeze. However, these 'supercooled' water droplets also continue to rise, until eventually they are so cold that they have to freeze.

From starting to form a cumulus cloud to the cell reaching 'maturity' may take less than 20 minutes. Even with oxygen, do not try to outclimb a growing cunim; the tops have been measured to grow at 5000 feet per minute.

FIGURE 5.1 THUNDERSTORMS

5.4   The Mature Stage

Once the rising air reaches its maximum altitude, usually the deep stable layer of the stratosphere, the cumulus stage is at its end. The air which is still rising continues to form cloud, probably on one side of the cell, but the air which has already risen is still saturated and the cloud spreads out. The frozen water drops start to descend, inside the mature cloud. Some fall to the ground as rain, but others are caught up in the rising air and climb again. These become larger and heavier as more and more water freezes around them. Eventually these also fall.

As these falling frozen drops, or hailstones for that is what they are, warm up below the freezing level they do not melt immediately. In fact many of them reach the ground still with frozen centres. These frozen drops absorb heat ("latent heat") from the air around them as their outsides melt, reducing the temperature of that air and bringing the freezing level in this mature cell down to the cloudbase. This same process also accelerates the updrafts by reducing the stability of the environment inside the cloud.

Although the actual mechanism is complex, in simple terms the rising hailstones and the falling hailstones passing each other produce static electrical charges, which tend to build up in different parts of the cloud. When the potential difference between two areas, either inside the cloud or between part of the cloud and the ground, reaches a critical stage, a spark (lightning) jumps between them.

At the top of the cloud, whatever water vapour remains in the rising air forms ice crystals directly instead of water drops (this is called "sublimation"). These ice crystals, being very light, can be supported by mild turbulence, and a sheet of cirrostratus drifts with the wind at the top of the cloud, into what is usually described as an 'anvil' shape (because that is what it looks like from the side). This 'anvil', visible in figure 5.1, is a characteristic of a cumulonimbus cloud.

At the bottom of the cloud, air is drawn in to the updrafts, but blown away from the downdrafts. Winds below the cloudbase may become exceptionally strong and gusty. Dust devils, water spouts or even tornadoes may form to mark particularly strong upcurrents, and bubbles of cloud (called "mammatus") may be pushed down by the downdrafts. Stratus cloud is also likely to form in the descending hail or rain.

5.5   The Dissipating Stage

The mature stage lasts for some time, but eventually the air at the bottom of the cell is cooled down too far to start rising. The remaining hailstones and water drops being supported by the updraughts now fall to earth. However, it takes time for them all to fall, and as they do they encourage more of the cloud droplets to form raindrops and so rain continues to fall for some time.

Eventually the cell contains only ice particles or cloud droplets. As the water droplets dissipate, or slowly fall as drizzle, the cell shrinks, leaving only the ice crystals in the anvil. However, as we have said, the cumulonimbus cloud contains many cells, at different stages of maturity, and so the storm itself may continue for a considerable time.

5.6   Airmass Thunderstorms

Thunderstorms generated by thermal convection tend to move on average with the wind at about 10,000 feet. The anvil drifting at the speed and direction of the wind at the tropopause may spread ahead of the main storm, reducing the sunlight reaching the ground there and thus reducing the heat energy to form cumulus cells. Airmass thunderstorms may therefore last for only an hour or so.

However, if the anvil does not block off the sun's energy, for example if the wind at the tropopause is in a different direction to the 10,000 foot wind, an airmass thunderstorm may continue for several hours. Because airmass thunderstorms generally start in mid to late afternoon, when diurnal heating is at its maximum, such storms may continue for an hour or so after dark (the cloud itself will bring darkness early).

In winter, a cold air mass originating in the arctic and flowing towards the UK in northerly winds may cause convection and airmass thunderstorms over the relatively warm sea. These may drift inland and produce heavy snowfalls.

5.7   Orographic Thunderstorms

Being triggered by air rising over sloping ground, these thunderstorms move in a similar fashion to an airmass storm. However, as one storm drifts away from the trigger, another storm is likely to start in the same place, drifting away in its turn to be replaced by yet another.

This apparently continous series of thunderstorms is likely to last for as long as the conditions of instability and moisture continue, although a change in wind direction may also remove the trigger.

5.8   Frontal Thunderstorms

If the two airmasses at a frontal surface are of different enough characteristics, the thunderstorms produced do not need solar heating as a trigger, and such thunderstorms are virtually continuous. The storms move in the same direction and average speed as the front itself, until the front weakens enough to stop the trigger action.

Warm fronts seldom produce thunderstorms, but cold fronts and cold occlusions often do. As mentioned in chapter 3, a group of thunderstorms is usually referred to as a "line squall", and such line squalls are frequently caused by frontal uplift.

5.9   Hazards associated with Thunderstorms

Thunderstorms contain very many hazards for aviators. The most obvious ones are listed below, but it must be emphasised that for the pilot of a light aircraft, a forecast of thunderstorm activity is a strong incentive to stay on the ground!

a.   **Lightning**

Lightning may strike an aircraft even outside the cloud. Aircraft designed for flight in cloud have all conducting surfaces electrically bonded together, so any lightning should pass through the structure with relatively little damage. However, many sport aircraft have no such bonding, and serious damage is likely. Glass fibre aircraft have suffered melting of control rods and even structural failure when struck by particularly powerful bolts. In any case, all electronic or magnetic equipment must be regarded as unreliable after a lightning strike, even if no damage is apparent.

b.   **Static Electricity**

Even without a lightning strike, the build up of static electricity in a cumulonimbus cloud may affect communication or navigation radios.

c.   **Vertical Currents**

The vertical currents in a mature cell are very strong, up to 3000 feet per minute. Even below the cloud the vertical currents can be very dangerous, sucking pilots up into the cloud or pushing them violently downwards on the final approach in what are called "microbursts".

d.   **Ice**

As we have seen, frozen water drops need a "nucleus" around which to form ice. If the nucleus is a dust particle, a hailstone is produced. An aircraft is an ideal nucleus, so ice will form readily around it. This ice changes the shape of the aircraft, causing a considerable loss of lift and increase in drag, so is a major hazard. It can form anywhere inside a cumulonimbus cloud, and will take a long time to melt afterwards.

e.   **Turbulence**

The high speed of the vertical currents, and the fact that an updraft may be close to a downdraft, causes a great deal of turbulence in and around the cloud, even as far as 15 to 20 miles downwind of it. Passengers have been injured and aircraft have suffered structural failure in such severe turbulence. In a light aircraft, the turbulence can lead to disorientation and loss of control.

f.   **Hailstones and Heavy Rain**

Hailstones hitting an airframe at high speed can damage the skin of leading edges (including windscreens), and even penetrate it. The noise of hail or even heavy rain hitting the airframe can be distracting to the pilot, as can any leaks into the cockpit. After the precipitation has fallen, runways may be flooded, resulting in longer stopping distances and possible loss of control on landing. The precipitation reduces visibility dramatically, and water on a windscreen can change the apparent aspect of a runway on final approach.

g.   **Windshear**

A more specific hazard of the up and down drafts is the resulting horizontal movement of the air close to the ground. Wind gusts into and away from the storm appear suddenly and from different directions, which can change through 180 degrees in seconds. On final approach, such wind changes, especially when coupled with the corresponding vertical currents, can easily result in a pilot over-running the runway, and the inertia effects can lead to loss of control. At large aerodromes, a 'windshear warning' may be broadcast. Unless you have NO other options, do not attempt to approach a landing field close to a cb.

h.   **Low Cloud**

The base of the cloud reduces as the hail melts and cold air descends. In addition, stratus or 'fracto-stratus' may form quite suddenly in the rain, preventing the pilot seeing obstacles or even the runway.

5.10   Warnings and Reports

If there is a chance of a thunderstorm occurring, most forecasters include the possibility in their forecast.   In clear air, 'isolated' thunderstorms or large cumulus clouds may be visible from a long distance and avoided, but if there is other cloud around, they may remain hidden and dangerous.   These 'embedded', and any forecast 'occasional', thunderstorms are best avoided in light aircraft by remaining on the ground.

Any met forecast or report which mentions thunderstorms or cumulonimbus cloud must automatically be assumed to warn of severe turbulence, icing, hail and the other hazards mentioned.   Such clouds should be treated as lethal and avoided by a considerable distance.

Intentionally Left Blank

1.   Which of the following is not a hazard to be expected in a thunderstorm?

     a.   Severe turbulence
     b.   Static electricity
     c.   Heavy rain
     d.   All the above are hazards to be expected

2.   Which of the following is not a hazard to be expected under a cumulonimbus cloud?

     a.   Hail
     b.   Severe icing
     c.   Strong downdrafts
     d.   All the above are to be expected

3.   Which of the following is incorrect about developing cumulonimbus cells?

     a.   The top of the cloud may grow upwards at 5000 feet per minute
     b.   Severe icing is likely
     c.   Heavy rain may cause turbine engine 'flame-out'
     d.   All of the above are true

4.   Which of the following is incorrect about thunderstorms?

     a.   They are composed of cells at different stages of development.
     b.   They will only last for about 20 minutes
     c.   They may form at a cold front
     d.   All the above are true

5.   Conditions favourable for cumulonimbus development are

     a.   steep environmental lapse rate and high dew point?
     b.   steep environmental lapse rate and low dew point?
     c.   low environmental lapse rate and high dew point?
     d.   low environmental lapse rate and low dew point?

6. Where in a cumulonimbus cloud should severe icing be expected?

      a.   In the anvil
      b.   Anywhere above the forecast freezing level
      c.   Above 10,000 feet
      d.   Anywhere in the cloud

7. In the event of a suitable trigger action to provide initial lifting, a thunderstorm is likely to develop in ...

      a.   Moist air, unstable through a deep layer?
      b.   Moist air, stable through a deep layer?
      c.   Dry but conditionally unstable air through a deep layer?
      d.   Dry air in an anticyclone?

8. What is the best action for the pilot of a light aircraft to take if thunderstorms are forecast?

      a.   Stay on the ground
      b.   Study a radar picture and choose a route avoiding any currently active storms
      c.   Study a lightning strike display and choose a route avoiding any recent strikes.
      d.   Rely on being able to see the storms and avoid them.

Chapter 6

Icing

6.1 Introduction

Airframe icing was introduced in the last chapter. Although hopefully sport pilots will have little contact with airframe icing, its effects are so severe that very few light aircraft are allowed to enter conditions where even light airframe ice may occur.

The chapter also includes information on engine icing. Intake icing, especially at the carburettor, is frequently encountered in light piston engined aircraft over the United Kingdom, and is a major factor in many aircraft accidents.

6.2 Ice formation

If water is brought to a temperature below freezing, it will try to turn to ice. However, unless there is some form of nucleus around which the ice can form, the water will tend to remain in a liquid state, called "supercooled". We discussed ice forming around dust particles to become hailstones in the last chapter. If an airframe is present, that provides a more than adequate nucleus, and the airframe itself becomes surrounded with a block of ice.

As some of an individual "supercooled" water drop changes into ice, heat ("latent heat") is released. This in turn warms up the water in the rest of the drop immediately surrounding the ice particle. Eventually the temperature of the remainder of the drop rises above freezing, and it flows past onto the rest of the airframe. The colder the airframe (the ice nucleus), the more ice forms at the instant the drop hits it and the less flows on. The cold airframe then cools the water down below freezing again, and more ice forms, in turn warming the remainder, and so on.

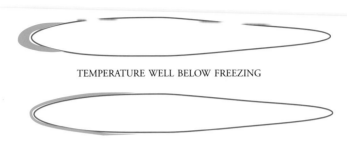

TEMPERATURE WELL BELOW FREEZING

TEMPERATURE JUST BELOW FREEZING

Fig 6.1 Ice formation at different temperatures

Supercooled droplets falling as freezing rain onto a static object will produce a sheet of ice over it. An aircraft in flight will hit the water drops with all its leading edges, which is where the ice will start to form. If the surface temperature is only just below freezing, most of the drops will flow back across the airframe, covering a large area, while at lower temperatures the leading edges themselves suffer nearly all the effect.

6.3   Rime Ice

Where the very cold water drops freeze rapidly, small amounts of air are trapped among the ice, producing a white, "opaque" effect. The slower the freezing, the more light passes through the ice (the more "translucent" it is). Very slow freezing ice forms as a virtually clear film over the surface, very difficult to see, like the "black ice" which sometimes forms on road surfaces.

If the airframe warms up in air temperatures above freezing (descends into warmer air), the surface of the ice starts to melt. Clear ice tends to "cling" to the surface on which it has frozen, and melts very slowly. However, any trapped air pockets allow the melting ice to break off in small lumps, and opaque rime ice melts quicker in the same air temperature than translucent rime.

6.4   Rain Ice

If the water drops themselves are a little above freezing, but meet a frozen airframe, the ice which forms spreads over a large area, is totally clear, and very difficult to see and to remove by warming. The worst case of this situation occurs when rain falls from a warm air mass (above 0°C) onto an aircraft which is either flying or attempting to take off in a colder air mass whose temperature is below freezing. This "rain ice" can be found under the sloping frontal surface between the air masses at a warm front or warm occlusion..

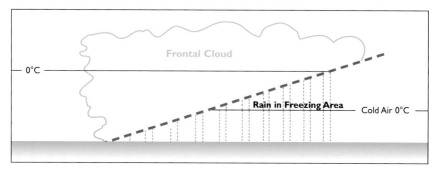

FIGURE 6.2   RAIN ICE HAZARD AT A WARM FRONT

6.5   Effects of Airframe Ice

The formation of ice adds mass to the airframe. The extra mass in turn affects the aircraft's balance. However, weight and balance effects are small compared to the aerodynamic consequences of icing. The ice changes the shape of the leading edges of the wing and tailplane, producing a considerable reduction in lift and increase in drag at both. This in turn reduces the aircraft performance and affects its handling, and invariably increases the stalling speed. The more ice is present, the greater the effect.

6.6   Removal of Airframe Ice

Some sophisticated aircraft have systems to prevent or remove airframe ice. An "anti-icing" system is designed to prevent ice, a "de-icing" system is intended to remove it once it has formed. However, most light aircraft have neither, and must not fly in icing conditions. If any icing is encountered, the pilot must act quickly to minimise the build-up.

Rime ice only forms in cloud. To prevent such ice forming, stay out of cloud. To remove ice which has already formed, however, the pilot must descend into warmer air, provided it is safe to do so.

If a pilot encounters rain ice, he must immediately try to fly away from the icing conditions. Turning back towards air in which no rain was falling previously, ideally directly away from the front, is usually the best course of action. Once clear of the rain, again a descent into warmer air, if possible, is the only means of removing the ice.

Even after a descent, as already explained, rain ice or clear rime ice may take a long time to melt. Ice avoidance is much safer than attempting ice removal after the event!

6.7   Reporting of Airframe Ice

Warnings of light, moderate or severe icing are given in aviation weather forecasts, and apply in any cloud above the freezing level (the level at which the air temperature is below 0°C). Rain ice should always be assumed to occur under every warm front if you are flying in air with a temperature below freezing.

6.8   Icing Clouds

Cumulonimbus clouds include the danger of severe icing. Any cumulus cloud can be expected to produce at least moderate icing on an aircraft which flies through it at an altitude above the freezing level.

Although icing will occur in stratus cloud if the temperature is below freezing, it tends to be light, unless the cloud is thick, especially around hills or as nimbostratus at a warm front. However, stratocumulus is more of a problem, particularly if the freezing level is between the cloudbase and and the top. Moderate and even severe icing can be expected near the top of such cloud. Cloud formed as a result of mountain wave activity, "lenticular" (lens shaped) cloud, officially called "altocumulus lenticularis", is actually high altitude stratocumulus, where the same effect is likely. Any pilot qualified to fly in cloud must note the forecast freezing level, but should also be aware that the freezing level varies in mountain wave, and drops to the cloud base in cumulonimbus.

6.9   Hoar Frost

As frost may occur on cold ground after a clear night, it may also appear on a cold airframe. Frost, like dew, forms as moist air cools below its saturation (dew) point. If that saturation point is below freezing, the water drops formed immediately freeze into individual ice particles. Hoar frost can also occur in flight if a cold airframe descends into warmer air and cools the air in contact with it to below its dew point.

Hoar frost looks relatively benign, and many pilots mistakenly believe that it will blow off the airframe. The ice particles tend to cling to the airframe on which they have formed. They also disturb the airflow just like any other form of ice, and like any other ice must be cleared completely from (as an absolute minimum) all lifting and control surfaces before flight. Windscreens and windows should also be cleared to prevent internal misting or frosting as the occupants' breath condenses onto the perspex.

6.10   Propeller icing

Propellers are aerofoils, and like any airframe surface may suffer icing. Propellers have specific problems, especially as ice starts to melt and chunks of ice may be thrown outwards by the rotating propeller. This may cause damage to any part of the airframe which these chunks hit, but the greater problem is likely to be the unbalancing effect of the remaining ice.

6.11   Engine intake icing

Like any other part of the airframe, the air intakes to an engine or its systems (for example the oil cooler) may suffer from icing. This "impact ice" may form at the curved surfaces around the intake, or on any protective grid which may be fitted over it. The ice may become so thick that the flow of air through the intake becomes restricted. Depending on the intake being blocked, this may reduce engine power output or increase engine or oil temperature beyond safe limits.

Ice may form inside the intake ducting. At any point where the ducting becomes narrow, the speed of the air flow increases, reducing its temperature. Any ice already forming becomes more severe, and the cooling may also bring the temperature of the air below both its dew point and the freezing point, allowing ice to start forming even in clear air at an ambient temperature (temperature of the surrounding air) above freezing.

6.12 Carburettor Icing

In a carburettor, aviation fuel is added to the air flowing into the cylinders. The mixing of the fuel with the air reduces the air temperature, which has already been reduced in the venturi built into the air passage to encourage the fuel to flow into it. If this reduction brings the air temperature below dew and freezing point, ice will form in the passages, restricting the flow of air. The restricted air flow reduces engine power, and often causes the mixture in the cylinders to become too rich, producing rough running. It may even prevent enough air reaching the cylinders to maintain combustion, causing the engine to stop.

The ice may form at any power setting. However, a carburettor also incorporates a throttle "butterfly" valve to alter the airflow and control the engine power. If the throttle butterfly is fully open, no extra restrictions are placed on the flow, but at low throttle settings, the valve closes. This restriction further lowers the temperature, by 20°C or more when the throttle is completely closed, and encourages ice to form in the carburettor, producing the effects described above much more quickly. Any carburettor heating system must be used to warm up the carburettor before the throttle is closed, and left on at all times when low power settings are selected, or when high humidity is experienced, for example in or near cloud or drizzle. It should also be used to warm the carburettor at frequent intervals.

Warm air can hold more water vapour than cold air, so if the air temperature is around or just below 20°C, severe carburettor icing is likely when the throttle butterfly is almost closed during a descent. A summer's day which combines such a temperature with moist air may be the most dangerous time for the condition. Figure 6.3 shows the conditions conducive to carburettor icing.

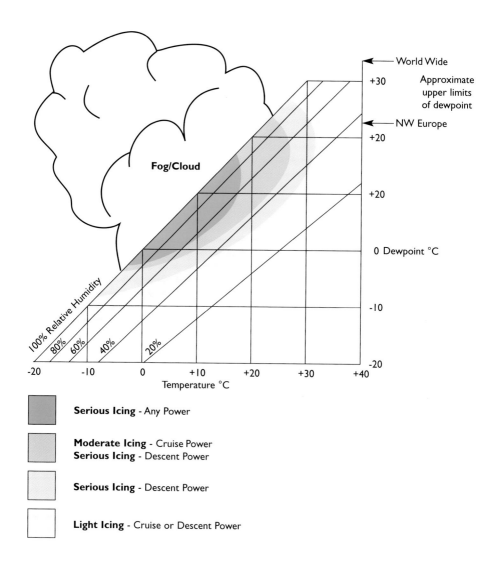

FIGURE 6.3 CONDITIONS FAVOURING CARBURETTOR ICING

Intentionally Left Blank

1.   Which of the following is true when water turns to ice?

   a.   Heat is absorbed from the air around the ice
   b.   Heat is released into the air around the ice
   c.   Heat is absorbed from the water itself
   d.   No heat transfer takes place

2.   When ice forms on an aerofoil, which of the following is correct?

   a.   At very low temperatures, the ice forms mainly at the trailing edge
   b.   At very low temperatures, air is trapped in the ice and makes it opaque
   c.   Both a and b are true
   d.   Neither a nor b are true

3.   Which of the following types of airframe ice is most likely to clear quickly in warmer air?

   a.   Rain ice
   b.   Opaque rime ice
   c.   Translucent rime ice
   d.   Clear rime ice

4.   Where is rain ice most likely to form?

   a.   Under the freezing level in the cold air before a warm front
   b.   Above the freezing level in the warm air behind a warm front
   c.   Above the freezing level in the cold air before a warm front
   d.   Under the freezing level in the warm air behind a warm front

5.   Which of the following is not a possible hazard of airframe icing?

   a.   Control problems
   b.   Loss of performance
   c.   Increased stalling speed
   d.   All the above are possible

6. During your pre-flight checks you find your aircraft is covered in hoar frost. What is the minimum area of the airframe which must be cleared of frost before you fly?

    a.   No frost need be removed
    b.   The leading edge of the wings
    c.   The leading edges of wings and tailplane
    d.   Every lifting surface

7. Which of the following conditions is most likely to produce serious carburettor icing in clear air at 2000 feet over the United Kingdom?

    a.   Climbing in summer at full power
    b.   Descending in summer at idle power
    c.   Climbing in winter at full power
    d.   Descending in winter at idle power

8. Which of the following conditions is unlikely to produce carburettor icing?

    a.   Cruising 200 feet below cloud, outside air temperature +2°C
    b.   Descending at idle power in clear air, outside air temperature +17°C
    c.   Climbing in cloud, outside air temperature -2°C
    d.   All are likely to produce carburettor icing

9. When flying below cloud, in drizzle at an air temperature of +5°C, which of the following is a risk?

    a.   Rain ice
    b.   Rime ice
    c.   Carburettor ice
    d.   There is no risk of icing

Chapter 7

Visibility

7.1 Introduction

As pilots, we need to see a certain distance ahead and around us in order to fly safely. 'Visibility' is basically a measurement of how far we can see if there is no solid object in the way. If the air consisted of pure gases, we should be able to see an infinite distance, and the visibility would be infinite (as we would expect in space). However, we have seen that water drops may remain in suspension in the atmosphere, and we looked at the formation of fog. Other things may become suspended in the atmosphere, such as the dust particles around which water drops or ice particles form, and such "particulates" (dust or smoke particles) also have an effect on the visibility.

Visibility in aviation is defined in one of several ways, depending who is reporting it and why it is being measured. "Surface visibility" is the maximum distance an observer on the ground can differentiate shape. It is measured in all directions, and averaged out to give a reported "prevailing visibility".

"Flight visibility" is the visibility forward of the cockpit of an aircraft in flight, at whatever altitude and heading it may be at the time. "Runway visual range" (unlikely to be of interest to sport pilots) is a measure of visibility along a specific runway, from a pilot's eyes on round-out.

7.2 Light Effect

The human eye detects light falling onto it, and because we do not look directly into the sun, we are always observing reflected light. When the sun's rays strike a water drop or a particulate, the light is further reflected and refracted (scattered) by them. It is much more difficult to observe shapes when we are looking towards the sun and the light is being reflected and refracted away from us, than when looking away from the sun when the light is being reflected back towards our eyes. Unless the sun is completely hidden from us by clouds, visibility is therefore almost always worst when

73

looking towards it. Approaching towards a low sun in the evening can be an actual hazard, especially if looking through a scratched or dirty windscreen.

FIGURE 7.1 APPROACHING TOWARDS A LOW SUN

7.3   Visibility Definitions

Fog is defined as visibility below 1000 metres. When visibility is reduced by water droplets, but is still 1000 metres or more, we call that "mist". When visibility is reduced by particulates, but is still 1000 metres or more, we call that "haze". We may find a visibility of 6 km described as 'haze' if particulates are present.

7.4   Radiation Fog

As described in chapter 2, radiation fog forms when moist air is cooled by contact with the ground which has radiated its heat into space, usually overnight. We saw in chapter 4 that cold air tends to move downhill overnight, so valley floors are susceptible to the formation of radiation fog if the surface wind is light (between 2 and 8 knots, approximately). This is especially true if the ground is wet, as in many river valleys. However, radiation fog may form anywhere if conditions are right.

It may thicken (the fog top may rise) as wind strength increases (perhaps diurnally in the morning) and may also drift with the wind away from its place of formation. This may affect an aerodrome where there was no fog at the start of the day. If the wind drops after radiation fog has formed, the fog will remain.

Radiation fog can be 'dispersed' (cleared) by an increase in wind (which will usually just 'lift' it into low stratus), or an increase in surface temperature above the dew point. The sun's rays will usually increase the temperature as the day advances. However, if a layer of cloud moves between the fog and the sun, or perhaps in winter the sun's rays are too weak to reach the surface through the fog layer, the fog may not disperse at all, or at best the visibility may increase only marginally.

7.5   Advection Fog

"Advection" comes from Latin words meaning "coming towards".   Although radiation fog may travel as described above, this is not 'advection' fog.   Radiation fog is caused by radiation, advection fog is caused by air moving from one place to another.

Advection fog forms when relatively warm moist air arrives over a cold surface, cooling the air in contact with it to below its dew point. This often occurs when an air mass which started life over a warm sea (a 'tropical maritime' air mass) arrives over either colder sea, or a land mass which has cooled in winter, perhaps being covered in snow.   It can happen at any time in the right conditions.

Around the British isles, such advection or "sea fogs" form in the South West approaches when a tropical maritime air mass arrives from the Azores over the cooler water around Wales and Cornwall, frequently drifting along the English Channel. However, the North Sea is generally colder than the Atlantic Ocean, so sea fogs are at least as common just off the eastern shore of England and Scotland. Especially in spring or early summer, sea breezes may bring sea fog towards the shore and over the land.

An increase in wind will 'lift' radiation fog into stratus. However, strong winds over a cold surface only serve to increase the amount of warm air in contact with that surface, so advection fog can and does form and continue in very strong winds. The process continues while the moist air remains in contact with the cold surface, so the fog will not disperse until the air mass moves away. If sea fog has come onshore with a sea breeze, it may be drifted offshore again by an overnight land breeze, but the fog will remain.   Advection fog almost invariably needs a cold front to change the air mass.

7.6   Hill Fog

In chapter 2 we looked at orographic cloud, and the formation of hill fog as that cloud touched the hill side. It is not intended to duplicate that description here, except to emphasise that orographic cloud invariably has a lower base, and is thicker, than cloud found over nearby flat ground. However, an aviation forecast may not use the expression "hill fog"; "cloud covering hills" is more usual, and is a valid description of the actual hazard to aviation.

7.7   Water and Visibility

Cloud particles, like fog, reduce visibility, and the thicker the clouds the lower the visibility inside them. The flight visibility inside clouds is academic, because even the thinnest cloud prevents a pilot flying by visual references. However, larger water drops also reduce visibility. In general, the larger the drop, the less the reduction, for example drizzle drops, being only slightly larger than cloud droplets, can reduce visibility dramatically more than larger raindrops, and can also prevent pilots flying by visual reference. Ice particles and hail reduce visibility more than rain but usually less than drizzle. Snow however is invariably worse.

Aircraft in flight are moving forward at speed, and the apparent movement of water drops towards the pilot (especially onto a windscreen without the wipers to be found on motor cars) attracts the pilot's eyes and causes an even greater reduction in flight visibility than surface visibility. It is important to remember this when reported surface visibility is poor in precipitation - flight visibility will be even worse.

7.8   Atmospheric Stability

In an unstable atmosphere, any convection spreads the particulates upwards and therefore reduces the number of them in a given volume of air, increasing the visibility close to the surface. The particulates are ideal centres for raindrops, and when these fall the air becomes 'clean' and visibility is good. Stable air, by contrast, keeps the particulates close to the earth's surface. The stability of the atmosphere varies as altitude increases, and even in a generally stable air mass diurnal heating tends to produce a shallow layer of unstable air close to the surface. The mechanical turbulence we looked at in Chapter 2 which produced stratus cloud also produces an effectively unstable layer. Whether caused by turbulence or convection, the unstable layer containing haze or even mist particles between the surface and the stable (or inversion) layer above it is commonly referred to as a 'haze layer'.

A haze layer tends to become shallower as the stable air above it deepens with time, for example in an anticyclone. The stable tropical maritime air of a depression's warm sector also retains the particulates and the drizzle droplets which tend to form around them below the stratus layer, reducing visibility in two ways. A similar effect may produce "frontal fog" just before the passage of a warm front.

Visibility above the haze layer is invariably considerably better than inside it. However, as can be seen in figure 7.4, the visibility from an aircraft inside the layer to the ground reduces as its height increases. In fact, there will usually be more particulates at the top of the layer, reducing the visibility there even further.

FIGURE 7.3 HAZE

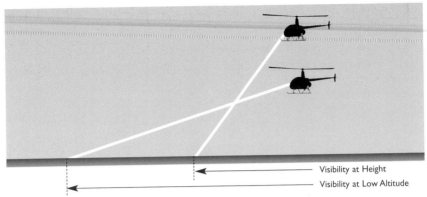

Visibility at Height
Visibility at Low Altitude

FIGURE 7.4 AIR-GROUND VISIBILITY WITH HEIGHT

In figure 7.5, however, we can see that if the aircraft climbs above the haze layer air-ground visibility will actually increase with height. Since flight visibility will also be very much better than when inside the haze layer, it can be seen that if it can be achieved, flight above the haze tends to be generally safer as well as more pleasant, although visual navigation may not be very easy.

FIGURE 7.5 VISIBILITY ABOVE THE TURBULENCE LAYER

FIGURE 7.6 FLIGHT ABOVE A HAZE LAYER

1. Which of the following is correctly described as "the visibility forward of an aircraft in flight"?

    a.   Runway visual range
    b.   Flight visibility
    c.   Surface visibility
    d.   Air to ground visibility

2. What is correctly described as "surface visibility reduced by water droplets to below 1000 metres"?

    a.   Mist
    b.   Haze
    c.   Fog
    d.   Cloud

3. If radiation fog forms, which of the following circumstances is most likely to clear it?

    a.   An increase in surface wind to 7 knots
    b.   A reduction in surface wind to 1 knot
    c.   Cloud forming above the fog layer
    d.   Diurnal solar heating

4. If advection fog forms, which of the following is most likely to clear it?

    a.   Surface wind increasing to 15 knots
    b.   The passage of a cold front
    c.   Diurnal solar heating
    d.   Cloud forming above the fog layer

5. A haze layer has formed between the surface and 2000 feet. At which of the following heights will flight visibility be greatest?

    a.   100 feet
    b.   600 feet
    c.   1800 feet
    d.   2400 feet

6. A haze layer has formed between the surface and 2000 feet. At which of the following heights will air to ground visibility be greatest?

    a.   100 feet
    b.   500 feet
    c.   1200 feet
    d.   1900 feet

7. In which direction will the surface visibility be least on a sunny winter's day at midday?

    a.   Looking North
    b.   Looking South
    c.   Looking West
    d.   Visibility will be the same in all directions

8. Which of the following are conditions suitable for the formation of radiation fog?

    a.   No wind, full cloud cover, over high ground
    b.   Strong wind, coastal aerodrome, cumulus cloud
    c.   Light wind, cloudless night, high humidity
    d.   Dewpoint below freezing, moderate wind, warm surface.

9. Advection fog may form ...

    a.   Over a warm sea when cold air flows over it
    b   Over snow covered land when warm moist air flows over it.
    c.   When the atmosphere cools at night
    d.   In the lee of high ground on a summer's evening

10. Which of the following can be expected to give the greatest reduction in visibility?

    a.   Moderate rain
    b.   Drizzle
    c.   Hail
    d.   Snow

Chapter 8

Charts

8.1   Introduction

Weather charts are available in several different forms. Television brought them into our homes, and the internet has increased the variety and quality of the information contained in the charts now freely available. With study and care, a pilot can gain a considerable amount of information from even the simplest of charts, but there are specific charts produced for pilots by the Met Office. This chapter is intended to guide pilots in understanding those charts most readily available to them.

The web site of the UK Met Office (www.metoffice.gov.uk) provides a considerable amount of information, including specialist aviation material. Anyone can obtain that material from the site, after a simple and free 'registration' process on the site itself. Information more detailed than the basics needed for safety is available if you wish to subscribe to it. Other web sites provide weather information, which in many cases has originated from the UK or another country's official met office site, although that information may not be as up-to-date or as complete as that on the 'official' site.

8.2   Synoptic charts

'Synoptic' charts are those which show the pressure distribution at the earth's surface, or to be more precise what the pressure would be if the surface was at sea level. Synoptic charts which show what the forecaster (or his computer) expects the sea level pressures to be at a future time are more correctly called 'forecast' charts. The Met Office web site provides a sequence of synoptic charts to indicate recent and forecast changes to the pressure patterns.

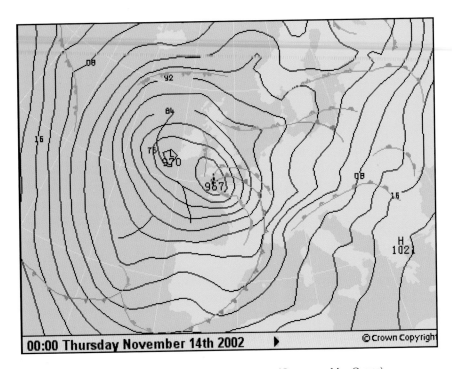

00:00 Thursday November 14th 2002 ►

FIGURE 8.1 A DEPRESSION ON A SYNOPTIC CHART (COPYRIGHT MET OFFICE)

As mentioned in chapter 3, the gradient wind may be measured by forecasters (and deduced by pilots) from the direction and distance between isogonals on a synoptic chart. The position of fronts at the surface are also marked, as shown in figure 8.1. Warm fronts have 'bumps' drawn on them (⏚⏚⏚⏚), cold fronts have 'spikes' (▲▲▲), and occluded fronts have a mixture of both. The fronts move in the direction of the symbols, hence up the page in both these examples.

Pilots can obtain an idea of future trends from the synoptic chart. Fronts tend to move at right angles to their surface position. Cold fronts travel at the geostrophic wind speed as measured between the isobars at the front, but warm fronts and most occlusions travel at about 2/3 of that speed. Depressions generally move in the same direction and speed as the geostrophic wind in their 'warm sector' (between the warm front and the following cold front).

8.3 Form 215

Weather forecasting is a science (although at times it may seem to be an art!). Although pilots need a knowledge of basic principles, they are not expected to make their own forecasts, and the local met office provides area forecasts for them. In the UK the "form 215" covers conditions below 10,000 feet. The British Isles and surrounding area is divided by 'scalloped' lines into zones where different weather conditions may be experienced, as in figure 8.2. The weather expected in each zone is described in simplified form. The charts are valid for periods of 9 hours, with the boundaries between zones shown close to the mid time of the forecast validity (for example 1200 if the forecast is between 0800 and 1700). Any movement of a zone boundary or a front is indicated by an arrow on the relevant lines showing the direction of movement and speed in knots.

The forecast for each zone is given separately. The descriptions start with the general conditions to be found in the zone, in the order visibility and significant weather, then cloud type and amounts with expected bases and tops above mean sea level. After the general conditions, any expected differences in either time (for example "gradually becoming between 1500 and 1800" or area (for example "near coasts") within the zone are given. Any differences which are expected to occur over a short time or a small area are described as "occasionally" (OCNL), while those expected to be limited in both time and area are described as "isolated" (ISOL). A light aircraft is unlikely to be able to avoid "occasional" weather deteriorations, but if visibility is good and the pilot has freedom to make track changes, he may be able to avoid "isolated" conditions.

Warnings about weather hazards which may be encountered, such as icing, turbulence, or strong winds, are listed. It should be noted (as written on the form) that any mention of cumulonimbus cloud (Cb) should be automatically taken to include warnings about severe icing and turbulence.

The chart uses standard international shorthand and symbols, and most descriptions used are fairly simple to interpret. Some are explained on the form itself, or in the booklet "GETMET" published regularly by the Met Office with the assistance of the CAA. Others such as "NW" for "in the North West of the zone" are relatively obvious, but a few may give problems. Part of the reason is that the codes are truly international, and include shorthand versions of more than one language. An alphabetical list of all those expressions used in written forecasts and reports is given at paragraph 8.8.

An area forecast is intended to warn of the worst conditions that the forecaster expects. Just because these conditions do not appear to be affecting his airfield, a pilot should not believe that the forecast is wrong. The worst conditions will usually be found between airfields, especially over high ground. It should also be remembered that forecasting is not an exact science. Even in a "correct" forecast, variations in frontal positions must be expected, and visibility may be up to 25% worse than the forecast suggests. Cloudbase (above sea level of course) may be 500 feet (or 25% of the published base whichever is greater) lower than forecast!

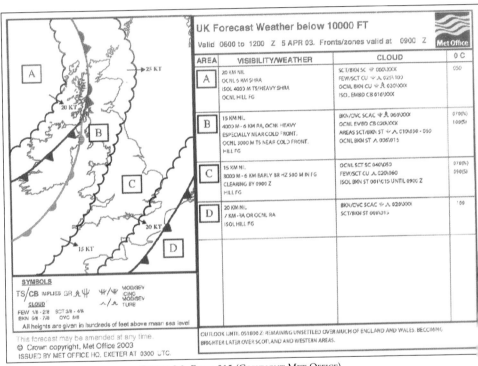

FIGURE 8.2 FORM 215 (COPYRIGHT MET OFFICE)

UK pilots wishing to fly outside the boundaries of United Kingdom airspace may obtain met form 415, an area forecast chart which covers the near continent in a similar fashion to the form 215 for the UK. Weather zones on the F415 tend by definition to be larger than on a F215, so less detail should be expected. However they are most useful when flying to a European destination. At this point we should mention that an aviation forecast should be obtained from the met office in the country of departure. International agreements frown on pilots contacting their home met offices when abroad, although there may be occasions when a pilot will consider it essential.

8.5   Other Significant Weather Charts

The Met Office produces a variety of charts for different purposes. Other countries also produce different charts, many of which are available on web sites. Although the form may be different, the information will still be presented in accordance with international procedures, and the symbols can be interpreted if you understand the principles behind them.

8.6   Chart Symbols

The following are used frequently on weather charts, and you should be able to recognise them, or at least have a copy of them available for reference, such as GETMET.

Symbol	Meaning	Symbol	Meaning
⌒	Moderate Turbulence	⬭	Mountain Waves
⌃	Severe Turbulence	⑊	Wind from direction of the tail, speed 25 knots (10 kt per long feather, 5 kt per short feather)
⌣	Light Icing		
⌣	Moderate Icing		
⌣	Severe Icing	∿	Freezing Precipitation
Thunderstorms symbol	Thunderstorms (includes severe icing, hail & turbulence)	△▽ Or	Hail

8.7   Wind Charts

The Met office produces charts showing forecast winds at varying pressure altitudes and positions on Met forms 214 (for the UK) and 414 (for the near continent). These are particularly useful for navigation planning, and are produced every 6 hours. The information is valid for 6 hours.

These charts, like the form 214 shown in figure 8.3, generally consist of a map of the area covered, with boxes placed around that map listing the forecast winds and temperatures at selected altitudes. These boxes are marked with the latitude and longitude of the position above which the forecast applies, which do not always correspond exactly to the centre of the box on the map.

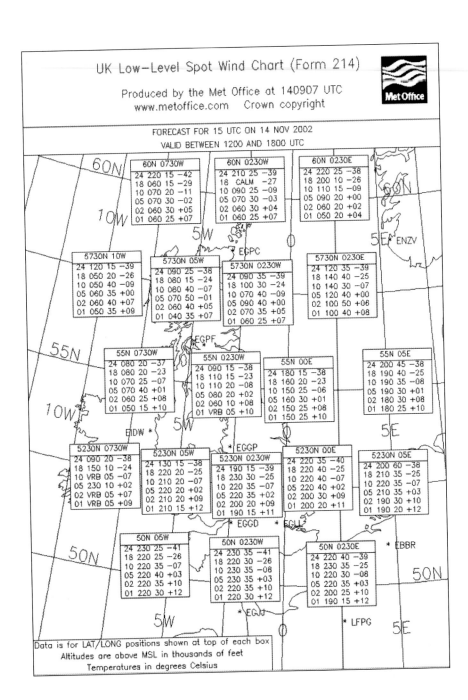

FIGURE 8.3 MET FORM 214 (COPYRIGHT MET OFFICE)

Flights seldom take place at a particular box, or even at one of the marked pressure altitudes. To use such a wind chart correctly, pilots ought to "interpolate" between the figures given at different altitudes and different boxes.

Sport pilots are unlikely to be particularly concerned about the exact temperature, but finding wind direction and speed requires two sets of calculations. We can see that the change of wind direction between 2000 feet and 5000 feet at 52°30'N 002°30'W is 20 degrees, so every 1000 feet the direction changes by approximately 7 degrees. The direction at 4000 feet will be 220-7 = 213°, and similarly the wind strength will be 35 - (35-20 = 15)÷3 = 35-5 = 30 knots.

If the position for which we require the wind and temperature lies between two or more boxes, we could make more interpolations. However, for practical purposes we can use either an area chart or a synoptic chart to decide which of the boxes is most appropriate for the flight, and use the figures from that box. For example, looking at the form 215 in figure 8.3, for a flight between Norwich and Bristol, the conditions in the box at 50°N 002°30'W would be appropriate, since the whole flight lies in the same airmass and changes are small. We should, however, still interpolate to find the wind at our intended pressure altitude.

8.8   Cross - Sections

Although not a chart as such, a forecaster may produce a picture representing the cloud and other phenomena expected during the day in the form of a "cross-section". Such pictorial representations of the weather forecast are useful briefing tools, and are drawn for particular places or areas. They are often used over the course to be flown in a competition.

The base line represents time. The height scale varies, giving more detail at low altitudes. The cloud pictures are drawn to provide representations of the expected amounts and heights of the layers above aerodrome or sea level as marked on the cross-section at various times during the day. For example, a cloud with a short base line represents a 'few' or 'scattered' amounts (as around 1100 hours in figure 8.4), while a longer line represents 'broken' cover and a continuous line represents 'overcast' or complete cover at that height. However, a lack of cloud marked at a particular time does not mean there is no cloud forecast for that time. The cross-section will normally have the details written on it in addition to the pictorial representation.

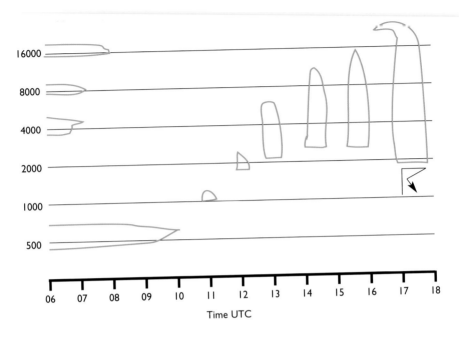

FIGURE 8.4 A CROSS-SECTIONAL FORECAST

8.9 Decodes of Expressions

So that pilots can recognise and interpret weather information wherever they are in the world and whichever agency has produced it, the shorthand expressions used in aviation forecasting have been internationally agreed. The Met office publishes a list of abbreviations used in aviation forecasts and warnings on its web site. Many expressions are obvious, but since some are not and most will appear on charts or forecasts, the list is reproduced here. The expressions in italics are less likely to be encountered in the UK or near continent, and are included mainly for reference.

ABV	above
AC	altocumulus
ACT	*active*
AS	altostratus
ASR	altimeter setting region
BC . . .	patches (followed by FG)
BEC	becoming
BECMG	becoming
BKN	broken (5 - 7 oktas)
BL	blowing (followed by DU, SA or SN)
BLO	*below clouds*
BLW	below
BR	mist
BTL	*between layers*
BTN	between
CAST	castellanus (towering AC)
CAT	clear air turbulence
CAVOK	cloudbase and visibility OK (military)
CB	cumulonimbus
CC	cirrocumulus
CI	cirrus
CIT	near or over large towns
CLD	cloud
CONS	*continuous*
COT	at or near coasts
CS	cirrostratus
CU	cumulus
CUF	*cumuliform (cumulus shaped)*
DIF	*diffuse (thin)*
DP	dew point
DR . . .	low drifting
	(followed by DU, SA, SN)
DS	duststorm
DTRT	deteriorating (becoming worse)
DU	dust in suspension
DUC	*dense upper cloud*
DZ	drizzle
EMBD	embedded (hidden)
EXP	expected
EXTD	extending
FBL	light (feeble)
FC	*funnel cloud (under CB)*
FCST	forecast
FEW	few (1 - 2 oktas)
FG	fog
FLUC	*fluctuating*
FM	from
FOQNH	*forecast QNH for a region*
FPM	feet per minute (vertical speed)
FRQ	frequent
FU	smoke

FZ	supercooled (freezing)
	(followed by DZ, FG, or RA)
GEN	generally
GND	ground
GR	large hailstones
GS	small hailstones or snow pellets
HPA	hectopascal (= millibar)
HVY	heavy
HZ	haze
IC	*ice crystals*
ICE	icing
IMPR	improving
INC	*in cloud*
INTSF	intensifying (getting worse)
INTST	*intensity*
ISOL	isolated
LAN	over land or inland
LOC	locally
LSQ	line squall
LYR	layer
MAR	over the sea (maritime)
MAX	maximum
MI . . .	shallow (followed by FG)
MNM	minimum
MOD	moderate
MON	over mountains
MOV	moving
MPS	metres per second
MT	mountains
MTW	mountain waves
MOV	moving
MPS	metres per second
MT	mountains
MTW	mountain waves
NC	not changing
NOSIG	no significant change expected
NS	nimbostratus
NSC	no significant cloud
NSW	no significant weather
OBS	observed
OBSC	obscured
OCNL	occasionally
OTLK	*outlook*
OVC	overcast (8 oktas)
PE	*ice pellets*
PL	*ice pellets*
PO	*dust devils*
PR . . .	banks of (followed by FG)
PROB	percentage probability

QFE	aerodrome level pressure		TC	*tropical cyclone*
QNH	*aerodrome elevation expressed as pressure altitude*		TCU	towering cumulus
			TEMPO	temporarily
QNH	sea level pressure		TL	until
			TROP	*tropopause*
RA	rain		TS	thunderstorm (may be followed by GR, GS, RA, SN)
RAFC	*regional area forecast centre*			
RAG	*ragged*		TURB	turbulence
RE . . .	recent (followed by phenomenon)		VA	volcanic ash
RMK	remarks		VAL	in valleys
RVR	runway visual range		VC . . .	in the vicinity (followed by phenomenon)
RWY	runway			
			VIS	visibility
SA	*sand in suspension*		VRB	variable
SC	stratocumulus		VSP	vertical speed
SCT	scattered (3 - 4 oktas)			
SEV	severe		WAFC	*world area forecast centre*
SFC	surface		WDSPR	widespread
SG	*snow grains*		WKN	weakening
SH . . .	shower (followed by GR, GS, RA, SN)		WRNG	warning
			WS	windshear
SIGWX	significant weather		WSPD	windspeed
SKC	sky clear		WTSPT	*waterspout*
SLW	slow			
SN	snow flakes			
SQ	squall			
SS	*sand storm*			
ST	stratus			
STF	*stratiform*			
STNR	stationary			

1. Which of the following is not shown on a "synoptic chart"?

    a.   A warm front
    b.   Isobars
    c.   Surface temperature
    d.   Surface pressure

2. Which of the following is not shown on an area forecast chart, such as the MET FORM 215?

    a.   Cloudbase above ground level
    b.   Pressure altitude of the freezing level
    c.   Coastlines
    d.   The speed of movement of a cold front

3. If a forecast chart uses the expression " MIFG ", what does this mean?

    a.   A shallow layer of mist will appear
    b.   Mist is expected to thicken into fog
    c.   A shallow layer of fog is expected
    d.   There will be patches of fog

4. If a forecast chart contains the expression "BCBR" what does this mean?

    a.   Becoming broken
    b.   Mist will form later
    c.   Visibility will be reduced in smoke later
    d.   There will be patches of mist

5. Using only the form 214 at figure 8.3, which of the following winds should you ideally use for a flight in the area of Bristol (EGCD) at 3000 feet at 5pm?

    a.   220/30
    b.   220/35
    c.   215/30
    d.   215/35

6. Using only the form 214 at figure 8.3, which of the following winds should you ideally use for a flight in the area of Wick (EGPC) at 3000 feet at 3 pm?

    a.   070/40
    b.   070/33
    c.   060/33
    d.   080/40

7. Which of the following need you not normally expect if you see the symbol on a chart?

    a.   Severe turbulence
    b.   Severe icing
    c.   Hail
    d.   Expect all of the above

8. What does the symbol ⌄ represent on a forecast chart?

    a.   Slight turbulence
    b.   Light icing
    c.   Moderate turbulence
    d.   Moderate icing

Chapter 9

Satellite & Radar Pictures

9.1 Introduction

Meteorological satellites have been orbiting the earth for many years. Photographs from them are mainly the tools of the professional forecaster, but they can be used by a pilot to assist in general understanding, as well as in interpreting the published forecast and whether it is going according to plan. Two types of satellite picture are generally available; infrared and visual.

Pictures are also available from ground based radar equipment. The signals from these radars are designed to reflect from water drops in the atmosphere, and so indicate the intensity of any precipitation. They are therefore usually called "rainfall radars".

Although both satellite and radar pictures are useful to pilots who understand them, they only show a limited amount of information, and are no substitute for a written aviation forecast.

9.2 Visual Satellite Pictures

Black and white photographs taken from satellites show sunlight reflected from clouds. Thin cloud allows much of the light to pass through, and appears grey, while thicker cloud appears white. A map of the ground beneath is overprinted on the photograph, with a grid of latitude and longitude. The published photographs are usually taken at midday when sunlight is at a maximum.

Figure 9.1 shows the continent of Europe below large patches of cloud. Far to the west of the UK, south of Iceland, we can see a large area of apparently small clouds (individual large cumulus or cumulonimbus clouds). The belts of more solid, greyish cloud surrounding it indicate frontal zones between that "polar maritime" air mass and warmer air masses to the East and West.

Above the western part of the UK the cloud is noticeable but fairly thin, indicating perhaps a weak front giving light if any rain. Over the eastern part of the country is an area of thin cloud, with clear skies around it. A similar, larger, area of thicker cloud covers most of France, and thick cloud centred above the Alps, stretching over Italy suggests the fronts associated with a depression.

The marking indicates it is a visual ("V") picture, taken at 1200 UTC on 18th November. The date is shown in the format used by many computers, with the month before the day.

FIGURE 9.1 VISUAL SATELLITE PHOTOGRAPH (COPYRIGHT MET OFFICE)

9.3 Infrared Pictures

To provide more information about the clouds, photographs are taken of the sun's reflected radiation at a lower frequency than that of light, in the infrared band. These reflections provide an indication of the temperature of the clouds reflecting them. The colder the cloud, the brighter the reflection. Ice clouds close to the tropopause show brightly, while the closer to the earth's surface, in general the warmer the cloud and the fainter the reflection.

Figure 9.2 shows the infrared picture (marked "I" for infrared) taken at the same time as the visual picture in figure 9.1. Here we can see that the thick cloud over the Alps is cold, indicating that the tops are at high altitude and providing more indication of the presence of a frontal depression. The clouds over France and eastern England are now shown as being at low altitude. In fact, a sheet of stratocumulus cloud covered France, and eastern England was under a layer of low stratus and fog.

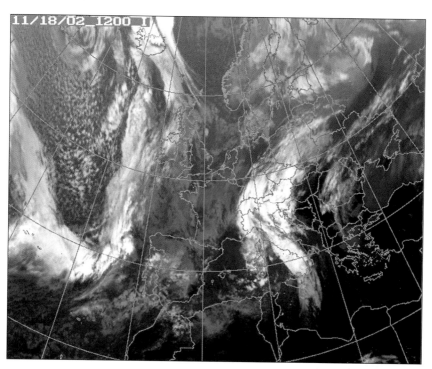

FIGURE 9.2 INFRARED SATELLITE PICTURE (COPYRIGHT MET OFFICE)

9.4   Rainfall Radar

A network of radar stations around the UK (and other countries) transmits signals which are reflected by water drops. Cloud droplets are usually too small to cause reflections, but drops large enough to form precipitation (whether actually falling or being supported in a cumulus or cumulonimbus cloud) will normally appear. In general, the larger and more concentrated the drops, the stronger the reflection.

These reflections or "returns" can be plotted on a map, to show the direction and distance of the reflecting drops from the radar transmitter. Computers assess the strength of the return against their range from the transmitter, and mark each return with a colour to indicate its strength. The maps are then studied by forecasters to identify the progress of fronts and storms, and even individual showers. Maps such as the one in figure 9.3 are available on the UK Met office's web site and are often shown on television forecasts. On that map, it may be noted that the date is shown in standard British format, with the day first.

In general, the strongest returns are shown in the brightest colours. Pale blue shows the weakest returns (suggesting the lightest precipitation), and the strength increases through dark blue, yellow, green, pink and red to white.

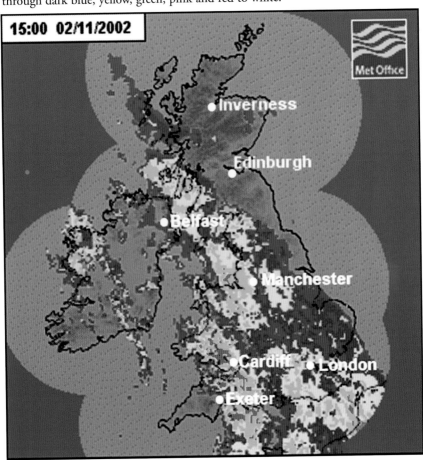

FIGURE 9.3 RAINFALL RADAR PICTURE (COPYRIGHT MET OFFICE)

Maps are published free of charge on the UK Met Office's web site every 30 minutes, and subscribers to the upgraded UK services can obtain more detailed ones every 15 minutes. Because forecasts are written far in advance, it is not always possible for the forecaster to be sure of the timing of any changes. Pilots can use the rainfall radar picture to see whether for example a front is slowing down or speeding up, producing any forecast change later or earlier than predicted. When used in conjunction with area and aerodrome forecasts and other information, these maps can provide valuable assistance to pilots. Decisions become easier; for example whether to set off early to complete a flight before worsening conditions arrive, or whether a delay would be likely to produce better weather later.

However, the radar picture only shows precipitation returns, not cloud. Cloud, especially low cloud, may form well ahead of any rain indicated on the picture, and drizzle droplets (often associated with low stratus) may be too small to show up as a return. The speed of movement of the weather phenomena producing the drops may also vary considerably as the terrain below it changes. Fronts or "bands of rain" are often slowed down as they pass over hills, but may speed up considerably when they reach flatter ground or stretches of water.

Intentionally Left Blank

1. Which of the following can normally be deduced from an infrared satellite picture?

     a.   The height of the lowest cloud
     b.   The altitude of the highest cloud
     c.   The amount of rain falling
     d.   The total cloud amount

2. Which of the following can be used as a substitute for a written aviation forecast?

     a.   An infrared satellite photograph
     b.   A rainfall radar picture
     c.   A visual satellite photograph
     d.   None of the above

3. Which of the following colours on a met office ground radar picture indicates the lowest cloudbase?

     a.   Red
     b.   White
     c.   Green
     d.   None of the above

4. Which of the following colours on a met office ground radar picture indicates the strongest precipitation?

     a.   Red
     b.   White
     c.   Green
     d.   None of the above

5. On figure 8.2, what is the altitude of the 0°C isotherm in the Northwest corner of the chart?

     a.   50 feet
     b.   500 feet
     c.   5000 feet
     d.   7000 feet

6. Using figures 9.1 and 9.2, what can be deduced about conditions over Norway on 18 November 2002?

    a.   There was no cloud
    b.   There was extensive low cloud
    c.   There was extensive high cloud
    d.   It was raining

7. Using figure 9.3, what can be deduced about conditions over Cardiff and Belfast at 3pm on 2 November 2002?

    a.   The rain was heavier over Cardiff
    b.   The rain was heavier over Belfast
    c.   There was no rain over Cardiff
    d.   There was no rain over Belfast

8. From figure 8.4, what hazards should you expect when flying at 1000 feet around 1700?

    a.   Hail
    b.   Heavy rain
    c.   Strong downdrafts
    d.   All the above are to be expected

Chapter 10

Reports & Forecasts

10.1 Introduction

Charts provide a general picture of a weather forecast, but cannot provide detail for a point or a small area. Met offices across Europe provide specific forecasts for most large aerodromes, so they require reports of the actual weather conditions at these aerodromes at specified intervals. These reports are produced either automatically by machine, or by trained observers.

It is usually convenient and practical for pilots operating from nearby, smaller, strips to use a combination of an area forecast and the aerodrome forecast for the major aerodrome to deduce what the weather conditions are likely to be at their own field. However, it is important to realise the limitations of that method.

10.2 TAFs

'Terminal Aerodrome Forecasts' or 'TAFs' are more accurate than an area forecast, and apply specifically to one particular aerodrome, taking into account local conditions (which may not apply to other nearby airfields). However, the possible variations listed in paragraph 8.3 still apply. They are produced by a central forecasting office a few hours before they come into effect. Most cover a period of 9 hours, although longer-term forecasts are available for major international airports.

The format is standard. After "TAF" comes the ICAO designator of the aerodrome, then the date and time the forecast was issued, then the period for which it is 'valid'. For example: "TAF EGLL 270450Z 2706/2715" means a forecast for London Heathrow issued on the 27th at 0450 UTC for the period 0600 to 1500 UTC on the 27th.

After the preamble comes the forecast itself. First the surface wind (true direction and knots), then the prevailing visibility in metres with any significant weather phenomenon, then a list of the cloud amounts and base heights in hundreds of feet moving upwards from ground level. For example: "23015G25KT 8000 -RA FEW008 BKN025" means a surface wind of 230° true averaging 15 knots with gusts to 25 knots, visibility 8 kilometres in light rain (-means light, +means heavy) with a few patches of cloud with base at 800 feet and almost complete cover of cloud with a base at 2500 feet above aerodrome level.

Wind variations may be in direction as well as speed, and may be described something like "250V310". Visibility of 10 km or more is given as "9999", visibility of less than 50 metres as "0000". The only cloud type mentioned will be cumulonimbus if forecast, written after the appropriate base height above the aerodrome, as "SCT1200CB". "NSC" may be used instead of the cloudbases if no cloud is expected below 5000 feet (and no CB or TCU in the area). "CAVOK" may replace both visibility and cloud if in addition to NSC, visibility is forecast to be more than 10 km.

After the main forecast comes a list of any changes expected during the forecast period. Either the period for or during which the change is expected, as "2710/2712" meaning between 1000 and 1200 UTC on 27th, or a specific time, such as FM271200 (from 1200 on that day), starts the secondary forecast. Then whatever the changes are expected to be; if any individual part of the forecast is not expected to change then it will not be mentioned. For example "PROB40 2710/2712 9999 BECMG 2713/2715 4000 DZ SCT012 OVC030" means 1) there is a 40% probability that during the period between 1000 and 1200 visibility will increase to 10 kilometres or more; 2) at some time between 1300 and 1500 the weather will deteriorate to a visibility of 4000 metres in drizzle with scattered cloud base 1200 feet and complete cover at 3000 feet (and not improve again during the forecast period).

10.3 METARs

A 'METeorological Aerodrome (think of it as "Actual") Report' or 'METAR' is produced normally every half hour, at twenty minutes after and ten minutes to the hour. These are in a similar format to the TAFs, although there are slight differences. Pilots should always consult the latest METARs to check that the TAF (which was issued some time previously) is correctly forecasting the conditions. If the METAR shows conditions worse than forecast for the particular time, we should expect worse conditions than forecast throughout the TAF period!

The report starts with the word METAR, the aerodrome designator and the time at which the observation was made. "METAR EGNJ 181150Z" indicates the report from Humberside airport at ten minutes to midday UTC on the 18th. Surface wind is followed by visibility, with RVR if appropriate, then any significant weather description. For example "25015G23KT 220V280 0900 R21/1200 -SNSH" is a report of a wind which has been gusting between 7 and 23 knots from directions varying between 220° and 280° true (remember runway directions are magnetic!), with a reported visibility of 900 metres, and a runway visual range on the approach to runway 21 of 1200 metres in a light snow shower. If there were major variations in visibility in any particular direction, these could be shown as for example "0900NW5000" if visibility was considerably better looking Northwest.

Cloud is again given as "few", "scattered", "broken" or "overcast" with the reported or measured base of each significant amount. The only cloud types mentioned are cumulonimbus and towering cumulus (which are likely to become cumulonimbus). For example "SCT003 OVC008CB" indicates less than half cover at 300 feet above the aerodrome with complete cover at 800 feet.

The surface temperature and dew point in degrees Celsius are then reported, followed by the QNH. For example "00/MS01 Q988" means an air temperature of zero and a dew point of minus 1 degree Celsius (high relative humidity), and setting a pressure of 988 hectoPascals on the sub-scale of an altimeter on the ground at the aerodrome will indicate the aerodrome elevation (above sea level).

Finally, any weather phenomena which have recently occurred will be reported, together with any warnings in force. For example, "RE+SN WSRWY21" indicates that heavy snow has recently been falling, and that windshear has been reported on the approach to runway 21.

As an addition to the weather report, the state of the runway or navigation aids may be included.

10.4 SPECIs

If the conditions change considerably between the half-hourly METAR reports, the Met office will issue a "SPECIal aerodrome report" at a different time. This follows the same format as a METAR, but is prefixed by for example "SPECI EGNJ 181210Z" to indicate that it is a special report. Pilots asking an Air Traffic Service Unit for weather information will be passed the latest METAR or SPECI and the time it was reported.

A continuous broadcast of the latest reports is available for some aerodromes. Major airports provide a terminal information service (ATIS) on published frequencies, often also available by telephone. "VOLMET" radio transmissions contain reports from a group of aerodromes, and the VOLMET frequencies are listed on CAA charts.

10.5 Landing Forecasts

Some major aerodromes and helicopter landing sites may have "landing forecasts" published. These are more accurate than TAFs, being issued much closer to the time for which they are actually valid. Private pilots may meet one of these landing forecasts if there is an addition to a METAR or SPECI in the form of a "TREND".

A TREND is a short term forecast, describing changes which the forecaster expects to happen during the next 2 hours, in the same format as a TAF. For example, the complete METAR for Humberside which we looked at above in paragraph 10.3 may well have been: "METAR EGNJ 181150Z 25015G23KT 220V280 0900 R21/1200 -SNSH SCT003 OVC008CB 00/MS01 Q988 RE+SN WSRWY21 BECMG 30012KT 9999 SCT018", if the forecaster expects the low cloud and weather to pass by and the wind to settle down, perhaps after the passage of a cold front. The part from "BECMG" is the TREND. The expression "NOSIG" is a TREND indicating that no change in conditions is expected.

10.6 Route Forecasts

Pilots may obtain specific forecasts for their route from their state's met offices, and most commercial flights do so. Private pilots may wish such a forecast if contemplating a long flight. A request to the UK Met Office for a "special forecast" requires 2 hours notice for flights less than 500 nm and 4 hours notice for flights greater than 500 nm.

10.7 Area Forecasts

Not everyone is able to understand, or in some cases receive, charts. The UK Met office produces area forecasts for specific parts of the country in written form, called 'Airmet' forecasts, which may be transmitted by telephone or fax. Other countries do the same.

In several countries, specific GA area forecasts called "GAFOR" are produced for General Aviation pilots. These assess how likely the pilots are to be able to fly under Visual Flight Rules. In the case of Germany, the country is divided into small areas, and each of these is allocated a code to describe in simple fashion the conditions expected (O = "open", M = "marginal", X = "closed" - visual flight impossible). Other countries have chosen to issue GAFORs for specific routes rather than areas.

Intentionally Left Blank

Use the following TAF for Cardiff to answer questions 1 to 7

TAF EGFF 120430Z 1206/1224 30008KT 3000 FU FEW015 TEMPO 1206/1209 0600 MIFG GRADU 1211/1213 6000 SCT020 PROB30 8000 BECMG FM121800 3000 FU BKN015 BECMG 1222/1224 OVC012 -RA

1. How long is the TAF valid for?

    a.   6 hours
    b.   12 hours
    c.   18 hours
    d.   24 hours

2. What should you expect the reported visibility to be at 12 midday?

    a.   600 metres
    b.   3000 metres
    c.   6 kilometres
    d.   8 kilometres

3. What weather is expected at 8 am?

    a.   Shallow fog
    b.   Fog patches
    c.   Nil with a 30% chance of fog patches
    d.   Smoke or possibly shallow fog

4. What reported visibility should you expect at 5 pm?

    a.   600 metres
    b.   3000 mctres
    c.   6 kilometres
    d.   8 kilometres

5. How much cloud, and with what base above the aerodrome, should you expect at 8 pm?

    a.   Complete cover at 1200 feet
    b.   Half cover or less at 1500 feet
    c.   Half cover or less at 2000 feet
    d.   Less than complete cover but more than half cover at 1500 feet

6. When and how much rain is expected during the period of the forecast?

    a.   Light rain starting at 10 pm
    b.   Moderate rain starting at 10.24 pm
    c.   Heavy rain starting at 10 pm
    d.   Light rain starting sometime between 10 pm and midnight

7. At what time should a private pilot aim to arrive at Cardiff with the best chance of being able to make a safe approach?

    a.   6 am
    b.   9 am
    c.   midday
    d.   3 pm

Use the following METAR for Newcastle to answer questions 8 to 11

METAR EGNT 071550Z 27008KT 9000 FEW028 19/13 Q1014 BECMG 04510KT 6000 BKN015

8. What is the time (GMT) of the report?

    a.   Quarter past 7 in the morning
    b.   Quarter past 7 in the evening
    c.   Ten to 4 in the afternoon
    d.   Ten to 6 in the afternoon

9. What is the surface wind at the time of the report?

    a.   8 knots from the west
    b.   8 knots from the east
    c.   10 knots from the Southwest
    d.   10 knots from the Northeast

10. When is the cloudbase likely to drop below 2000 feet above the aerodrome, and how much of that cloud will there be?

    a.   One to two oktas of cloud is already below 2000 feet
    b.   One to two oktas will form at ten to five
    c.   More than half cover is already below 2000 feet
    d.   More than half cover will form at any time in the near future

11. What is the air temperature at the surface?

    a.   10°C
    b.   13°C
    c.   14°C
    d.   19°C

Use the following report for Prestwick to answer questions 12 to 14

SPECI EGPK 221850Z 29005KT 3000 HZ SCT008 06/06 Q1002 GRADU 0800 BKN003 TEMPO 0400 VV///

12. What atmospheric pressure is being reported?

    a.   A sea level pressure of 1008 hPa
    b.   A sea level pressure of 1002 hPa
    c.   A pressure on the aerodrome of 1008 hPa
    d.   A pressure on the aerodrome of 1002 hPa

13. What is expected to happen to the cloudbase?

    a.   Sometime soon, it will drop to 300 feet, but will at times be impossible to measure
    b.   At 8 pm, it will drop to 300 feet, then soon afterwards become impossible to measure
    c.   Sometime soon, it will drop to 800 feet, then later to 300 feet
    d.   Sometime soon, it will drop to 600 feet

14. What is the reported relative humidity?

    a.   40%
    b.   60%
    c.   80%
    d.   100%

Intentionally Left Blank

Chapter 11

Weather Recognition

11.1 Introduction

While an understanding of an aviation forecast is important, forecasts cannot always be particularly accurate. To fly safely, pilots need to be able to detect such inaccuracies, especially if the weather is becoming worse than forecast. While several hints have already been dropped in previous chapters, some more guidance is given here. It should help pilots recognise the approach of deteriorating weather, hopefully before they actually fly into it.

There are some characteristics which pilots should expect from certain situations, and we shall look at these first. A synoptic forecast chart, or a TV forecaster's comments, can prepare you for them.

11.2   General Assessment - Air Mass

The air mass which is forecast to affect your route will bring certain types of general weather. With its relatively high humidity at low altitudes, a tropical maritime air mass over the UK will generally be stable, with poor visibility. If associated with the warm sector of a depression, there will often also be low stratus cloud and possibly drizzle, although visibility above the turbulence cloud layer may be good (if the pilot can fly there). If associated with an anticyclone in summer, the conditions are likely to be either clear skies or a sheet of stratocumulus cloud (which is often difficult to forecast). Advection fog is also possible. Returning polar maritime air will give similar conditions, but probably not so pronounced.

Tropical continental air seldom reaches the UK. However, when it does, conditions are likely to be stable. There will be a deep and thick haze layer, with little cloud. If a cold front moves it out of the way, dust and even sand may fall in the raindrops.

Polar continental air may arrive in winter, and is often the cause of "cold snaps" of clear skies and overnight frosts. Visibility is generally good except in the showers (often sleet or snow) from the moisture it has collected on its travel across the North Sea. Being unstable, any cloud will be cumulus type, but often restricted (with the showers) to the Eastern coastal areas.

The commonly seen polar maritime air is again unstable, with good visibility outside precipitation, but the moisture it has collected on its passage across the Atlantic tends to produce much more cloud. In summer, the cloudbase may be high and the cloud "fair weather cumulus", but especially in winter frequent, possibly heavy showers from deeper cumulus are likely. Thunderstorms are also possible if a suitable trigger exists. In winter, cumulus may be found over the sea and coastal areas even when the land is too cold to produce convection.

If arctic maritime air is forecast, the wind will be Northerly and very cold. Cumulonimbus will form over the sea and drift a short distance over land, probably dropping snow over coastal areas. Visibility outside showers will be excellent, but any snow encountered will reduce it dramatically.

11.3   Pressure Patterns

Anticyclones produce settled weather. However, that means that the air becomes progressively more stable, and surface visibility will become steadily worse (and the inversion at the top of the haze layer lower) unless the air mass changes. Cloud may not exist, but especially in winter stratocumulus cloud may form daily, dispersing at night. In summer, with no cloud (or thin cumulus) temperatures may increase daily and slow down the visibility reduction, but in winter the clear skies may lead to radiation fog which takes longer to clear each day.
Ridges tend to be shorter lived than anticyclones, so although the weather will again be settled for a time, the disadvantages are less likely to take effect.

Depressions move quickly, and their effects are mainly those of their frontal systems already described. However, even without a frontal system marked on a chart, the centre of the depression is generally marked by thick convective clouds with few gaps between them, and often showers with a low cloudbase.

Troughs are often fronts which a forecaster has difficulty categorising. Bands of showers or periods of continuous precipitation are common, and especially over or near high ground may produce considerable cloud at low altitudes.

11.4 Constructive Report Reading

Even though you may have made a general assessment of the likely conditions before flight, you will never have all the information which a forecaster has, and you must never try to do without his expertise. You must check not only the area forecast for your route, but also TAFs and METARs for all aerodromes you expect to pass, and any which might be useful as diversion aerodromes. Be sure you know everything that the forecaster expects to happen.

However, the forecaster will only tell you what he (or to be precise his computer) thinks is most likely to happen. He will seldom be able to tell you what he thinks might happen if events turn out slightly different. You can prepare yourself by actively looking for suggestions that the forecaster thinks that may be the case. Look carefully at the forecasts for any "PROBs", since they give such an indication. "TEMPO", "OCNL", and even "ISOL" will almost certainly affect your flight, as will any gusts in the forecast wind. We should always be ready to divert to another airfield if we cannot land at our intended destination, but take note of the possible weather problems and know where you can divert to if these problems actually occur. Carry enough fuel to get there and try a circuit or two before having to land.

Using an area forecast and a map, it is easy to compare the expected cloudbases with the elevation of the ground over which you intend to fly, to ensure you have plenty of clear air between them. Note the wind direction and strength. In addition to affecting your navigation track, a wind blowing up a slope is likely to produce upcurrents and low cloud on and above that slope, with corresponding downcurrents on the other side.

For safety, always expect the forecast to be about 30% worse than it is written. If the wind is forecast to be near your crosswind limit (including any forecast gusts), be ready to fly to a diversion with a runway much closer to the wind. If the cloudbase is a little low, either avoid high ground altogether, or plan alternative route legs over low ground which you can change to if necessary. Carry enough fuel to fly the alternative route.

If visibility is not very good, plan your route so that the best navigation features are always down sun from you. That suggests you should approach your destination from the direction of the sun. If you can, select a flying altitude above the haze layer. If you expect to arrive at your destination when the sun is low in the sky, check the forecast wind and available runways to try to avoid landing into sun.

If your route takes you downwind, you will be flying into weather which was recently over your departure point. You know what the forecast said; take note of exactly what the recent actual weather was at your departure point and compare the two. Ask pilots who were flying earlier what the conditions were. If the actual weather was worse than forecast, so will be the weather along your route.

11.5 Cloud Patterns seen from the Ground

Even from the ground, clouds can provide information about the weather beyond them. The old saying "red sky at night - shepherds' delight" suggests the upper cloud at the downwind side of a cold front reflecting the setting sun's rays. The converse "red sky in the morning - sailors take warning" suggests the cirrus cloud of an approaching warm front reflecting the rising sun's rays.

There are of course more indicators of an approaching warm front, with its associated lowering cloud, increasing wind and precipitation (sometimes freezing rain) than just a red sky. Increasing amounts of thickening upper cloud are the classic sign of an approaching warm front. However, few fronts exhibit classic signs, and clouds seldom build up progressively from above. More frequently small amounts of stratiform cloud will appear in bands, often lenticular in form, well in advance of the surface front. Even the rain which often arrives some fifty miles before a surface warm front tends to come in surges rather than in a progressively increasing amount. Figure 11.1 shows a sky with a warm front approaching from the direction of a range of hills which has broken up the theoretical cloud pattern.

FIGURE 11.1 A WARM FRONT APPROACHING

An approaching cold front is seldom visible, hidden by low cloud in the warm sector. However, when it has arrived, perhaps giving heavy rain, often a shaft of sunlight will be visible in the distance to indicate the clearance behind it. The actual passage of the cold front will be indicated by a characteristic veering of the surface wind as the air temperature and dew point drop, even if the sky does not immediately clear.

Especially in frontal zones, cumulonimbus clouds are sometimes "embedded" (hidden by other clouds). However, individual distant cunims will often be indicated either by the cirrus cloud of an anvil, or by towering cumulus with considerable vertical extent, which will themselves turn into storm clouds. Cumulus type cloud at high altitudes, the classic "altocumulus castellanus" clouds, are another type which may turn into cumulonimbus in the near future.

11.6   Cloudbase Estimation from the Ground

It is often difficult from the ground to detect the height of the cloudbase above. If there is no cloudbase measuring device on the aerodrome or strip, and reports from nearby aerodromes are unobtainable, it is often tempting to take-off and see what the cloudbase actually is. Pilots can frequently be drawn into believing that the area forecast is too pessimistic.

The first way that a pilot can judge cloud height is by looking at an obstruction in the area and seeing if and where cloud is touching it. However, experienced pilots can also estimate cloudbase by looking at patches of cloud drifting in the wind. The relative movement of the patches across an observer's view is a function of wind speed and cloud height. If a pilot regularly observes the cloud movement across the sky when he knows both the wind speed and cloud height, he will develop a skill in cloud height estimation, which he should practise and check on good weather days. Forecasts of gradient wind speed are usually more accurate than those of cloudbase, but in any case pilots should understand the relationship between the windsock at their local airfield and the actual wind strength (different windsocks have different indications). Fast moving cloud patches on a day of only moderate winds indicate very low cloud!

Even if you cannot remember how to make cloudbase calculations as in chapter 2, if you have access to temperature and dew point measurements, or humidity reports, remember that high humidity (temperature and dew point close together) indicates that cloud will form at very low heights.

Precipitation can also indicate a lowering of a previously higher cloudbase. While rain often falls from relatively high cloud, drizzle drops are so close to cloud droplet size that drizzle may be regarded as a major indicator of a very low cloudbase. For that reason, as well as the reduced visibility and possible carburettor icing, a private pilot should not attempt a take off in drizzle.

11.7   Cloud Patterns from the Air

Once airborne, the same information is available as from the ground. However, more specific indicators exist once the aircraft is at its planned cruising altitude. Even without obvious cloud in sight as in figure 11.2, a pilot who looks well ahead and around can spot clues to possible problems.

FIGURE 11.2 CLOUD AHEAD AND BELOW

If the visibility is generally good, significant variations in that visibility around the horizon provide warning signs of either cloud dropping below the aircraft's present altitude, or precipitation falling in that area. Neither is good news for a private pilot. If seen early enough, the first option could be an altitude change to below the cloudbase if practicable (no lower than any obstacle ahead). If that does not provide a clear horizon, or if the problem is seen late, turn towards a clear area, perhaps behind you.

FIGURE 11.3 FIRST INDICATIONS

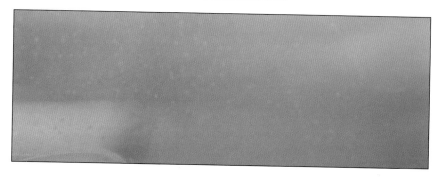

FIGURE 11.4 CONTINUING TOWARDS IT

The "curtains" of cloud which appear as in the left half of the picture in figure 11.3 indicate precipitation. Even if the horizon remains relatively clear for some time, the aircraft will be affected. Precipitation may spread quickly, especially around the base of a large cumulus, so be sure of having another safety option (preferably a diversion airfield in sight) before attempting to fly around precipitation from an overcast (or even broken) cloudbase. Cloud shape and movement can indicate other problems; curls or rolls of cloud suggest turbulent air.

In good visibility under large areas of cloud, the sun's rays striking the ground, or even shining through gaps, can provide an indication of how much cloud lies in a particular direction (even though visible sun's rays may come hand in hand with reduced visibility in that direction). This can help in planning possible route changes if the cloudbase starts to lower. A large area of sunlit ground in one direction may indicate a gap big enough to allow an aircraft to climb away from dangerously low cloud (small gaps may allow you to maintain a view of the surface below, but are unlikely to allow a safe climb). If the gaps are lined up across the wind, however, they are likely to be wave induced (see chapter 4), and an aircraft's rate of climb may be reduced in the gap, especially at the upwind end.

11.8 The Ground from the Air

It is important to always look at the ground as far ahead and around as possible in order to make navigation easy. However, it is also important in weather monitoring. We have discussed the significance of areas of significantly reduced visibility around the horizon. If flying above a haze layer, a general reduction in air to ground visibility suggests that once the aircraft has descended, the flight visibility inside the haze layer will also have reduced.

Low cloud or mist patches may appear in shallow valleys, giving warning of radiation fog ahead. In fact, any cloud which forms below an aircraft's cruising altitude should be treated as a potential hazard. Often the first low cloud will appear in hilly regions, but that may provide an indication that further cloud may form over flatter terrain. Patches of cloud close to cruising altitude indicate possible carburettor icing conditions, as does the top of a haze layer.

FIGURE 11.5 CUMULUS AT FLYING HEIGHT

While the forecast wind velocity is likely to be quite accurate, especially at cruising altitudes, it is important to be aware of any changes. We should always have an estimate of the local surface wind, not only in case a forced landing is required, but also as an indication of possible crosswind problems at the destination.

Wind strength is difficult to estimate, even from the movement of smoke, although if it becomes particularly strong dust or snow may be blown around, and the Beaufort Scale may be useful if flying over water (see chapter 3). However, the movement of cloud shadows across the ground can indicate the rough speed of the gradient wind, as can an aircraft's drift when flying crosswind, or groundspeed when flying into or down wind.

Direction is usually easier to determine. Smoke over the ground will indicate local surface wind. However, it is important to remember that if convection is taking place in generally light wind conditions, the surface wind at a particular time may be considerably different from the gradient wind, and may change rapidly as the convective currents change. This may be deceptive if attempting a landing in such conditions; a pilot may select an approach into the surface wind indicated by a single smoke column, only to find himself approaching from the wrong direction at touchdown. It may be better to remember the surface wind which was forecast and plan an approach accordingly, if necessary waiting until any local disturbances settle down.

FIGURE 11.6 SURFACE WIND INDICATION

If you cannot remember the forecast surface wind, or that which affected you on take-off, it is possible to determine the gradient wind by flying a steady turn through 360 degrees and seeing which way the aircraft drifts. Unfortunately, if the engine has already failed, one is unlikely to have enough time for such a manoeuvre! Try to remember (or calculate) the direction from which the sun will be shining when flying into wind.

However, if several sources of smoke indicate a surface wind different to that which one was expecting, a knowledgeable pilot will think of possible reasons for that difference. Is a front moving at a different speed to that forecast? Is a cumulonimbus cloud affecting the winds? Is there a valley funnel effect taking place?

11.9 Use of Radio in the Air

Many pilots prefer to talk to as few air traffic service units (ATSUs) as possible when flying, and several do not possess either a radiotelephony licence or a licensed aeronautical radio transmitter. This deprives them of a useful source of weather information. For example, the "information for safety of flight" which a Flight Information Service must provide, includes any METARs, SPECIs and TAFs which the pilot asks for. The controller or FISO may also have reports from other pilots in the area you intend flying to. In less than obviously ideal conditions, it is advisable to make use of the facility if you can. Since METARs change every half hour, it is a good habit to check those for the intended destination and possible diversion aerodromes at least at that interval. For the benefit of others, if you encounter unforecast poor weather in flight you may wish to use the FIS to pass on that information.

However, even without talking to an ATSU, pilots can detect changes in weather patterns by listening to appropriate stations (and a receiver does not need to be licensed). The 'VOLMET' facility is a continuous broadcast on published VHF frequencies of METARs and SPECIs from major aerodromes, and can usually give an indication that similar weather can be found at nearby airfields. Any 'TREND' given at the end of each report is a landing forecast and therefore more accurate than a TAF. A reduction in expected cloudbase or visibility reported by VOLMET may be an indication of general deterioration. A reduction in pressure (QNH, or RPS - regional pressure setting) usually indicates that weather is becoming generally worse. A surface wind which backs and increases earlier or later than the time forecast can even give a knowledgeable pilot warning of the increasing or decreasing speed of an approaching front or other forecast condition. Similar information may be deduced from the ATIS at any major aerodromes being passed.

Knowledgeable pilots are always prepared for problems which might arise in any of the situations we have described in this book. They use the available reports to confirm whether potential problems, even if the forecast does not include them, have either occurred or have become more likely. In summer, wind changes at coastal aerodromes will indicate the presence of sea breezes. In autumn and winter, the temperatures and dew points reported can provide useful indications of possible mist or fog, especially at low lying aerodromes, even before the visibility itself drops. Light winds in the lee of a ridge of hills while the gradient wind is strong indicate lee wave or rotor turbulence there and in the area.

As pilots, we have no control over the weather, so we need to make every effort to prevent it from causing us problems.

1.   A warm front is shown on the synoptic chart as approaching. The TAF for your aerodrome is as follows: 2506/2515 23015KT 9999 BKN020 OVC045 GRADU 2510/2512 7000-RA SCT008 OVC020 BECMG FM 251400 3000RA SCT004 OVC010. You arrive at the aerodrome at 0930, hoping to fly before the weather deteriorates. At that time, which of the following might indicate that the poor weather is likely to arrive earlier than forecast?

     a.   A surface wind of 210/20 kt
     b.   Light rain
     c.   5 oktas of cloud, base 1500 feet agl
     d.   Any of the above

2.   You are climbing in generally good visibility. The horizon in front of you becomes hazy while that to either side is still well defined. Which of the following are you likely to encounter?

     a.   Low cloud ahead
     b.   Rain ahead
     c.   Either (a) or (b)
     d.   Neither (a) nor (b)

3.   Cumulus cloud covers generally less than half the sky. In the distance a sheet of cirrus or cirrostratus cloud is visible. Which of the following would not be indicated by that?

     a.   A warm front is approaching
     b.   Thunderstorms are in the area
     c.   A cold front is retreating
     d.   Any of the above are possible explanations

4.   You are flying towards an aerodrome near London Gatwick. From which of the following sources would you not be able to obtain an updated aerodrome forecast for Gatwick?

     a.   London VOLMET South
     b.   London Flight Information Service
     c.   Gatwick Approach
     d.   It is available from all the above

Use the following TAF and METAR for February 21st to answer questions 5 to 10

TAF EGPF 2106/2115 14025KT 6000 SCT008 OVC015 GRADU 2111/2114 4000RA SCT004 OVC012 PROB30 TEMPO 2113/2115 1200+RA BKN002 OVC008

METAR EGPF 210950 13020G28KT 6000DZ FEW008 BKN012 OVC020 07/06 Q0998

5. What is the lowest cloud reported at 0950?

    a. Half cover or more, base 800 feet
    b. Less than half cover, base 8000 feet
    c. Quarter cover or less, base 800 feet
    d. 3 or 4 oktas, base 6000 feet

6. What is the maximum wind reported between 0940 and 0950?

    a. 28 knots from the Southeast
    b. 28 knots from the Northwest
    c. 20 knots from the Southeast
    d. 20 knots from the Northwest

7. What was the lowest cloud forecast for 0950?

    a. One or two oktas, base 800 feet
    b. 3 or 4 oktas, base 800 feet
    c. Half cover or more, base 400 feet
    d. 30% chance of half cover or more, base 200 feet

8. When is moderate rain forecast to arrive?

    a. Before 11 am
    b. Not before 11 am, but before 2 pm
    c. Not before 1 pm, but before 3 pm
    d. After 2 pm

9. What is the lowest cloudbase which a pilot should expect at 1.30 pm?

    a. 200 feet
    b. 400 feet
    c. 600 feet
    d. 800 feet

10. Which of the following would be the most likely VOLMET cloud report to be at 1020?

    a. FEW004 BKN008 OVC020
    b. FEW008 OVC020
    c. SCT010 BKN020
    d. SCT020

11. When a surface cold front passes, which of the following happens?

    a. The dew point rises and the surface wind veers
    b. The dew point rises and the surface wind backs
    c. The dew point falls and the surface wind veers
    d. The dew point falls and the surface wind backs

12. What conditions would you expect immediately after a cold front passes?

    a. An increase in visibility and a lowering of cloudbase
    b. An increase in visibility and an increase in cloudbase
    c. A reduction in visibility and a lowering of cloudbase
    d. A reduction in visibility and an increase in cloudbase

13. A tropical maritime air mass is covering the UK in winter. What flying conditions would you expect?

    a. Clear skies, unstable air with excellent visibility at low altitudes
    b. Low stratus cloud, with poor visibilty below but good visibility above it
    c. Heavy snow showers and thunderstorms over the North Sea and coastal regions
    d. A thick haze layer extending to high altiudes but little or no cloud

Intentionally Left Blank

Answers to Exercises

Chapter 1

1. b
2. c
3. b
4. b
5. d
6. c
7. c
8. b
9. d
10. c
11. c
12. c
13. b

Chapter 2

1. b
2. a
3. b
4. c
5. b
6. a
7. c
8. c
9. b
10. d
11. a
12. c
13. d
14. c
15. b

Chapter 3

1. a
2. b
3. c
4. c
5. b
6. a
7. d
8. b

Chapter 4

1. c
2. b
3. c
4. b
5. b
6. a
7. c
8. b

Chapter 5

1. d
2. b
3. c
4. b
5. a
6. d
7. a
8. a

Chapter 6

1. b
2. b
3. b
4. c
5. d
6. d
7. b
8. d
9. c

Chapter 7

1. b
2. c
3. d
4. b
5. d
6. a
7. b
8. c
9. b
10. d

Chapter 8

1. c
2. a
3. c
4. d
5. a
6. b
7. d
8. c

Chapter 9

1. b
2. d
3. d
4. b
5. c
6. b
7. a
8. d

Chapter 10

1. c
2. b
3. d
4. c
5. d
6. a
7. d
8. c
9. a
10. d
11. d
12. b
13. a
14 d

Chapter 11

1. d
2. c
3. d
4. a
5. c
6. a
7. b
8. b
9. a
10. a
11. c
12. b
13. b

Index

latent heat, 18, 55, 63
lee wave, 46, 120
lenticular cloud, 46, 47, 66
light effect, 73
lightning, 55, 57
line squall, 37, 57
lull, 37

M

mammatus, 55
mature stage, 55
mechanical turbulence, 77
METAR, 102, 113
microburst, 57
millibar, 6
mist, 74, 120
mountain wave, 66

N

navigation, 33
night effect, 34
nimbostratus, 24, 66
NSC, 102

O

occasional, 83
occlusion, 21, 36, 53, 57, 65
OCNL, 83, 113
okta, 24
opaque rime ice, 64
orographic, 19
orographic cloud, 16, 46
orographic thunderstorm, 53, 56
orographic uplift, 43
overcast, 25

P

particulates, 73, 74, 77
polar continental, 112
polar maritime, 22, 93, 112
precipitation, 24, 58, 77, 95, 116
pressure, 1, 5, 31, 34, 46, 120
pressure altitude, 7
pressure difference, 31
pressure gradient, 31, 35
pressure gradient force, 31
pressure reduction with height, 7
prevailing visibility, 73

PROB, 102, 113
propeller icing, 67

Q

QFE, 7
QNH, 7

R

radiation, 2, 4, 14, 20
radiation fog, 14, 73, 74, 112, 118
rain, 24, 48, 55, 58, 76, 114, 116
rain ice, 65, 66
rainfall radar, 93
red sky, 114
reflection, 73
refraction, 73
return, 96
returning polar maritime, 22, 111
ridge, 6, 45, 49, 112, 120
rime ice, 64, 66
rotor, 47
rotor streaming, 48, 120
rough running, 68
runway aspect, 58
runway state, 103
runway visual range, 73, 103
RVR, 103

S

saddle, 49
safety altitude, 46
SALR, 18, 19, 48
satellite, 93
saturated, 13
saturated adiabatic lapse rate, 18
saturation, 16, 18, 19, 48, 54, 67
scattered, 25
sea breeze, 38, 75, 120
sea fog, 75
severe icing, 83
showers, 24
sky clear, 25
smoke, 119
snow, 24, 56, 76, 112
SPECI, 103
speed of fronts, 36
spot wind chart, 85
squall, 37
stable, 46, 49